# A Study of Pragmatic Creativity in Non-native Speakers' Communication

# 非母语说话者的语用创新研究

吕丽盼◎著

華東理工大學出版社
EAST CHINA UNIVERSITY OF SCIENCE AND TECHNOLOGY PRESS
·上海·

**图书在版编目(CIP)数据**

非母语说话者的语用创新研究：英文 / 吕丽盼著.
—上海：华东理工大学出版社，2018.12

ISBN 978－7－5628－5597－2

Ⅰ.①非… Ⅱ.①吕… Ⅲ.①语用学-研究-英文
Ⅳ.①H030

中国版本图书馆CIP数据核字(2018)第223771号

**策划编辑** / 王一佼
**责任编辑** / 赵楚月
**装帧设计** / 戚亮轩
**出版发行** / 华东理工大学出版社有限公司
地址：上海市梅陇路130号，200237
电话：021－64250306
网址：www.ecustpress.cn
邮箱：zongbianban@ecustpress.cn
**印　　刷** / 江苏凤凰数码印务有限公司
**开　　本** / 890mm×1240mm　1/32
**印　　张** / 6.75
**字　　数** / 197千字
**版　　次** / 2018年12月第1版
**印　　次** / 2018年12月第1次
**定　　价** / 68.00元

# 内容摘要

非母语说话者的成功交际在一定程度上借助了交际过程中的语用创新来实现。本书拟从语用创新的概念出发，着力探讨非母语说话者在交际中如何借助语用创新实现成功交际的问题。

语言与创新的相关研究主要集中在语言创新和修辞创新层面，对语用创新的研究关注度相对较低。语言创新的研究主要以生成创新以及词汇创新为主，而语言创造性使用方面的研究则主要涉及语言的修辞创新，包括文学作品中的修辞及日常用语中的修辞。学者注意到母语说话者的语言创新在话语中具有使话语更有说服力、制造幽默交际效果或传达讽刺意味等功能，然而关于非母语说话者的语言创新功能方面的现有研究，特别是在话语层面却成果寥寥。除此之外，非母语说话者通过有限语言水平实现成功交际这一语言现象尽管非常普遍，在研究领域中的关注度却不高。

本书认为语用创新是指情境中的交际者在话语层面相互合作，从而巧妙地展开互动，建构话语并实现某种交际效果的语境化现象。基于此，本书进一步提出非母语说话者的语用创新是指情境中的非母语交际者在话语层面相互合作，从而利用有限的语言和文化资源，围绕非惯用的、创新性的表达或形式建构话语，实现成功交际的语境化现象。以社会认知方法为理论基础，在前人研究背景下，本书对“语用创新”这一概念提出以上新的理解。该方法作为跨文化语用学理论基础，同样适用于非母语说话者在交际中的语用创新研究。我们认为，语用创新具有如下特征：

1）语境关联性；

2）灵活性、主观性、个体性；

3）效果导向性等。

在语料方面，本书关注非母语说话者交际行为中的语用创新现象，重点搜集并整理了非母语说话者的自然口语语料。通过收集、转录并建立非母语说话者在自然状态下的会话和日常交际中的会话，结合 VOICE 语料库中的会话，共同作为本书的主要语料来源。借助社会认知方法，本书致力于分析情境中的非母语交际者如何在语境中通过相互合作，进行语用创新，从而实现成功交际，并对语用创新形式进行分类、整理与分析。

本书借助社会认知方法，对所收集的非母语说话者交际的语料进行分析，深入探讨非母语说话者如何在交际中利用语用创新的各种形式实现成功交际。基于对现有语料的分类整理，本书认为非母语说话者在交际中的语用创新形式主要可以分为三大类：

1）语法形式上的语用创新（包括改变句法特征、省略词汇语法特征等）；

2）词汇形式上的语用创新（包括切换词汇功能、使用其他替代词汇、描述词汇和创造新词等）；

3）搭配形式上的语用创新（包括改变介词短语搭配、改变动词短语搭配和改变套语表达的搭配等）。

在语料分析的基础上，本书提出假设：非母语交际的成功在一定程度上依赖语用创新的实现。非母语说话者在交际中使用语用创新的动因则包括：

1）交际需要（使用语用创新克服文化差异以及语言能力不足等困难，避免交际失败）；

2）积极的合作态度（区别于母语说话者的一般本能合作）；

3）为实现话语和情境一致所付出的努力（语言水平相对较低的非母语说话者在语言能力有限的情况下，为实现对等交际功所能付出的努力）。

基于社会认知方法，本书对语用创新研究提出了方法论指导，这也是对非母语说话者交际研究的进一步拓展。首先，语用创新的特征及对非母语说话者如何展示语用创新的探讨使得语用创新这一定义更加完善。其次，将非母语说话者在交际中的语用创新与母语说话者的语用创新进行区分，体现其特殊性。语用创新的形式探讨则对日常跨文化交际以及鼓励语言水平不足的学习者进入实际交际有着指导意义。最后,本书对跨文化语用学研究的进一步发展起了一定的推动作用,并提供了新的研究思路。

简言之,本书是对语用创新,特别是非母语说话者在交际中的语用创新的初步研究,其结论是开放性的,仍有广阔的发展空间。首先,尽管语言创新和语用创新之间的关联在书中有所提及,两者之间的继承和发展、区别和联系仍非常值得进一步探讨。此外,今后研究可以考虑建构完善的理论框架,将社会认知方法和非母语说话者在交际中的语用创新研究结合起来,并建立更加丰富、详实的语料库来进一步完善母语以及非母语说话者的语用创新形式研究。

# ABSTRACT

Taking the socio-cognitive approach as the theoretical foundation, this book aims at raising the hypothesis that pragmatic creativity plays an important role in non-native speakers' successful communication. This study intends to explore how non-native speakers achieve successful communication through pragmatic creativity.

Previous studies mainly focus on the creativity of language in use at the sentence level and on the creative aspect of language use at the utterance level. As for creativity of language use at the discourse level, little attention has been paid to it. The notion "linguistic creativity" refers to both generative creativity and lexical creativity, while the creative aspect of language use primarily refers to rhetorical features of both literary language and non-literary language. Some scholars are also interested in native speakers' efforts in seeking for a convincing, humorous or sarcastic effect in communication, but few of them discuss functions of non-native speakers' creativity of language use. Besides, little attention has been paid to how non-native speakers manage to achieve successful communication barely relying on their limited linguistic and cultural resources.

Pragmatic creativity refers to a contextualized fact that integrates situated speakers' creative use of language forms and other interlocutors' mutual cooperation to reach certain communicative aims at the discourse level. Therefore, pragmatic creativity that occurs in non-native speakers' communication is defined as a contextualized fact that integrates situated non-native speakers' creative inputs and other interlocutors' cooperative understanding, which aims to achieve successful communication. The socio-cognitive approach, adopted by Kecskes (2013a) as a valid theoretical foundation for intercultural pragmatic studies, also works well in understanding pragmatic creativity in non-native speakers' communication. Non-native speakers' pragmatic creativity shares the following features:

(1) situated relevance;

(2) flexibility, subjectivity and individuality;

(3) effect-orientation.

The corpus used in this study is from naturally occurring data. The data in this study consist of two parts. Some are recorded from naturally occurring conversations in a language-learning class as well as daily communication. The others are from the online corpus VOICE (Vienna-Oxford International Corpus of English), which is ready-made naturally occurring data. With the guidance of socio-cognitive approach, this study aims to analyze how non-native speakers achieve successful communication through pragmatic creativity with the support of data analysis.

Three forms of pragmatic creativity in non-native speakers' communication are discussed in great details with examples. They are pragmatic creativity in grammatical forms (including changing utterance structures and omitting lexico-grammatical features), pragmatic creativity in lexical forms (including shifting lexical function, using an alternative word, describing an intended word and creating a new word) and pragmatic creativity by deviating collocation (including deviating prepositional phrases in collocation, deviating verbal phrases in collocation and deviating formulaic expressions in collocation). Reasons for non-native speakers' creative uses in conversations are as follows:

(1) Communicative needs. The main aim of non-native speakers' input is to cooperate in order to achieve successful communication, and their pragmatic creativity is aroused by such an aim.

(2) Positive cooperative attitude. Different from native speakers' automatic cooperation, non-native speakers' cooperation is driven and active. Such an active cooperative attitude promotes non-native speakers to show their pragmatic creativity in communication.

(3) Creative but imperfect lingual-situational matching efforts. Non-native speakers' limited linguistic and cultural resources restrict them from speaking as native speakers do. Therefore, they will make imperfect lingual-situational matching efforts so as to convey what is required in the context for the interaction to proceed until the communication task is accomplished.

To sum up, with the guidance of the socio-cognitive approach, this book intends to enrich the understanding of creativity in language use as a matter of intercultural pragmatics. It not only expands the research scope of non-native speakers' communication, but also encourages speakers with relatively insufficient linguistic competence to take part in communication, and helps them to be pragmatically creative. This book is a preliminary research, which is about how non-native speakers achieve successful communication relying on different forms of pragmatic creativity during the process of intercultural communication. It is not yet mature and still far from perfect. On the one hand, the differences and similarities between pragmatic creativity and linguistic creativity is a topic worthy of further exploration. On the other hand, further refinement and a well-grounded research frame are needed to promote socio-cognitive approach to the analysis of pragmatic creativity in both native and non-native speakers' communication.

# Table of Contents

# Chapter One Introduction

How do non-native speakers understand each other's unconventional forms or components in utterances? It is a question that doesn't often catch the eye of linguists. Non-native speakers refer to those who speak a language other than their mother tongue when communicating with others. Unlike native speakers, non-native speakers are always in a disadvantageous position in communication, especially for those of comparatively lower language proficiency and who lack cultural information of the target language. In spite of the disadvantages, non-native speakers could still manage to overcome the difficulties most of the time.

Pragmatics focuses on studying language in context, and thus communication in real scenario naturally falls into the research scope. In traditional pragmatic studies, the four topics (deixis, presupposition, speech act, and conversational implicature) are its research interests, all of which focus on utterance in context. Besides that, other studies within the scope of pragmatics involve context as well. Intercultural communication is a new topic in the field of pragmatics. Kecskes (2013a: 1) points out that intercultural pragmatics varies from traditional and classic pragmatics in "its multilingual, intercultural, socio-cognitive, and discourse-segment (rather than just utterance) perspective", and the standpoint takes intercultural communication as "a normal 'success-and-failure' process rather than a collision of cultures". In his point of view, other factors should be taken into account instead of being limited to cultural differences and misunderstandings in intercultural communication. The roles of "prior and actual situational experience" as well as "common ground" have been emphasized in order to achieve successful communication. It is of vital importance to have a mutually built common ground so as to achieve successful communication and make other interlocutors understand in intercultural communication.

Taking non-native speakers in communication as the research object, this book aims to study the intercultural communication from the perspective of pragmatics. Our attention will be mainly focused on non-native speakers' pragmatic creativity in intercultural communication. Before we go into more details about pragmatic creativity, several points need to be made clear. First of all, there is the research background including a brief introduction to recent studies as well as the reason why this research topic is selected. Secondly, we will focus on the essential research questions, which is necessary and helpful for readers and scholars in this field to have a better understanding of its research value. Last but not least, we will establish the foundation of a valid research of great importance, and give a description of the data used in this study.

## 1.1 Research Background

Intercultural communication is an interesting topic even from the pragmatic point of view. Kecskes (2013a) points out that studies of intercultural communication should not only focus on cultural differences and misunderstandings, but also on other factors that stand in the way of successful communication for non-native speakers. They may come across various problems in communicating with others because of their limited linguistic and cultural knowledge.

Previous studies of non-native speakers' communication mainly focus on the following aspects:

(1) Comparing various conversational features between native speakers and non-native speakers (eg. Taleghani-Nikazm, 2002; Dings, 2012; Garcia and Terkourafi, 2014);

(2) Analyzing non-native speakers' conversations in pragmatic use (eg. Pavlenko, 2008; Osvaldsson, Persson-Thunqvist and Cromdal, 2013);

(3) Exploring non-native speakers' identity (eg. Kramsch, 1997; Park, 2012; Chung, 2014);

(4) Detecting native speakers' attitude toward non-native ones (eg. Flowerdew, 2001; Munro, Derwing and Burgess, 2010);

(5) Investigating non-native speakers' language skills (eg. Bohlken and Macias, 1992; Liu and Gleason, 2002; Pae and Greenberg, 2014);

(6) Others.

The research perspectives of previous studies range from non-native speakers' ability as well as their social status to the differences or gaps between native and non-native speakers. Lots of scholars in this area pay their attention to specific institutional conversations, such as Miranda warning, emergency call and so on. As for how non-native speakers achieve successful communication in intercultural communication, not much ink has been spilt to it, not to mention the fact that they are of low language proficiency.

Not only different cultural background but also low language proficiency can lead to the failure of communication or misunderstandings in non-native speakers' communication. In spite of that, it is not a rare thing that non-native speakers who encounter those problems could still manage to achieve successful communication. Therefore, what arouses our interest is how they manage to make it despite such a disadvantage. We hold the opinion that the secret lies in pragmatic creativity. With the guidance of socio-cognitive approach, pragmatic creativity refers to a contextualized fact that it integrates situated speakers' creative use of language forms and other interlocutors' mutual cooperation to reach certain communicative aims at the discourse level. Non-native speakers' pragmatic creativity refers to a contextualized fact that integrates situated non-native speakers' creative inputs and other interlocutors' cooperative understanding, which aims to achieve successful communication. Although pragmatics is generally about the study at the utterance level, this book intends to lead pragmatics research to a discourse level, in which successful understanding or communication is based on the mutual cooperation of situated interlocutors in discourse.

Creativity is not quite a new topic either in linguistics or in pragmatics. It has undergone a fruitful investigation by scholars from different perspectives. Linguistic creativity, first put forward by Chomsky (1972: 155), refers to "the recursive property to the syntactic component". His followers then defined such kind of creativity as generative creativity. Lexical creativity is also a kind of creativity in language. It usually comes with productivity, another feature of language. Within recent decades, scholars turn their attention to creativity in context. Thus, different factors, such as social and cultural elements, have been taken into consideration in analyzing communication. One thing we can be sure of is that studies of creativity in language are developing in an all-round way. The development of studies of linguistic creativity grows rapidly. The definition of linguistic creativity varies from one to another; so do research objects. Pragmatic creativity is also of no exception. Scholars such as Gumperz (Prevignano et al., 2003) and Paradis (2009) have discussed pragmatic creativity, a comparatively new term in pragmatics. Pragmatic creativity is known both as a "counterpart" (Paradis, 2009: 64) to Chomsky's linguistic creativity, and an "innovation in the context of certain constraints" (Prevignano et al., 2003: 25). Although this notion has already aroused the interests of some linguists, not that much discussion on pragmatic creativity is given, let alone pragmatic creativity in non-native speakers' communication.

In this study, we focus on pragmatic creativity in non-native speakers' communication at the discourse level, which is different from other pragmatic studies in which utterance has been taken as a basic research unit. It has been pointed out that intercultural communication is a process of "success-and-failure" instead of collision of cultures (Kecskes, 2013a). While for non-native speakers, successfulcommunication requires not only the context, but also mutual cooperation of all the interlocutors at presence, which is well supported by the socio-cognitive approach.

Socio-cognitive theory is first raised by Albert Bandura (1977), who studies how behavior is learned through social learning theory. He looks into the relation between a person's perceived self-efficacy and behavioral change, based on how a comprehensive theoretical framework for studying human behavior is established. From social cognitive view, human functioning or behavior is explained through "a model of triadic reciprocality", which constructs the interplay among behavior, cognitive and other personal factors as well as environmental events (Bandura, 1986:18). Human behavior is taken as the result of mutual influence of the individual and the environment. While in intercultural pragmatics, socio-cognitive approach supports that what is said, instead of human behavior, is under mutual influence of individuals and the environment. According to socio-cognitive approach, words or sentences that non-native speakers utter are influenced by situated interlocutors as well as the context.

Understanding what an interlocutor says should not be restricted to an utterance level but also at the discourse level. Therefore, in intercultural communication, non-native speakers' utterance in this process is "open and dynamic", and its understanding requires both conversational context and cooperation of other interlocutors.

Pragmatic creativity in this book is different from what other scholars define, since not much attention has been paid to the fact that how non-native speakers manage to achieve successful communication with their low language proficiency in intercultural communication. Socio-cognitive approach, which functions as the theoretical foundation for intercultural pragmatics, also works for understanding pragmatic creativity in non-native speakers' communication. We will take the socio-cognitive approach as the theoretical base to study non-native speakers' communication from the perspective of pragmatic creativity. Socio-cognitiveapproach explains such kind of creativity in language with a focus on intercultural communication. This book proposes the hypothesis that pragmatic creativity plays an important role in non-native speakers' successful communication through detailed data analysis.

## 1.2 Research Questions

The main purpose of an incompetent non-native speaker in intercultural communication is to get communication through. It has also been pointed out that pragmatics is almost equal to semantics for non-native speakers (Kecskes, 2013a). Therefore, how non-native speakers get communication through with their comparatively low language proficiency is what we are paying special attention to.

In this book, we will illustrate how pragmatic creativity helps non-native speakers get communication through. Before proceeding further, the following questions should be solved so that we can move to the detailed discussions:

(1) Does pragmatic creativity exist in non-native speakers' communication? If yes, what does it refer to?

(2) How does pragmatic creativity appear in non-native speakers' communication?

(3) How do we understand the way that pragmatic creativity works in non-native speakers' communication?

(4) Why are non-native speakers pragmatically creative in communication?

## 1.3 Data Collection

Our data focuses on how non-native speakers achieve successful communication. A non-native speaker, whose language competence is different from a native speaker's to a great extent, is someone who speaks other languages rather than his or her mother tongue in communication. Non-native speakers' communication can be understood in two situations. One is that only non-native speakers are engaged in communication. The other is that both non-native speakers and native speakers are involved in communication. Although whether native speakers take part in the communication or not could be used to classify different kinds of non-native speakers' communication, it is beyond our concern in this book. Thus, as long as a non-native speaker is involved in communication, it is what we mean by non-native speakers' communication. In the following sections, we will briefly explain what kind of data will be used in this book and then describe the sources of data in detail.

### 1.3.1 Source of Data: Naturally Occurring Conversations

There is a heated debate over whether task-oriented or

naturally occurring language data should be applied to intercultural communication studies. Task-oriented conversations, such as Discourse Completion Task, have been widely applied by scholars in the field of language acquisition to investigate the speech acts (Blum-Kulka, 1983), problematic, contextually-specific prompts (Zuskin, 1993), language learners' production (Jebahi, 2011; Aufa, 2014), and provide sociolinguistic data. Parvaresh and Tavakoli (2009) validate three kinds of discourse completion tasks, including "open written discourse completion task, dramatic written discourse completion task and discourse role play task". Among those three, open discourse completion task is the one that is least recommended. While for naturally occurring conversations, it is usually more spontaneous, during which process speakers may feel less controlled. This kind of data is what researchers are supposed to actually put more emphasis on, since this kind of data is more significant for researchers to study linguistic phenomena. The only problem is that it is not always easy to collect such kind of data due to various limitations. Moreover, for quite a number of linguistic researchers, if they focus only on naturally occurring data, the result may not come out as efficient as those in task-oriented conversations do. Therefore, task-oriented data often serves as a complementary method to naturally occurring data.

In order to distinguish those two kinds of data, we will make a comparison between the extract from House's (2009) study and the extract from the corpus of VOICE. The former is a study on EFL conversations among students at the University of Hamburg, which is collected through quasi-natural conversations. While the latter is collected from a meeting at the University of Vienna. After the comparison, Cogo and Dewey (2012: 30) found that speakers in task-oriented conversations seemed to be more constrained while speakers in naturally occurring conversations tended to be freer and more engaged in the conversations. We may take a look at the following two examples:

(1.1) A close friend gave you a package that you were supposed to give to someone else, but you found out that you lost it. Now, you met this close friend.

— Your close friend: Did you deliver the package?

— You: O brother forgive me.

(Jebahi, 2011: 658)

(1.2) S1: maybe we start (.) we start e:r (.) writing now and we shall:<9><un> xxx </un></9>

S4: <9> yeah just </9><1> make the thing <soft> <un> xx </un> yah </soft></1>

S2: <1> yeah and we don't need </1> even (.) to talk that much i mean if (.) w-we <2> have <un> xx </un></2>

S4: <2> we only </2> have like forty-five minutes we should REALLY <@> get started </@>

SS: yeah

S2: so you <fast> (go ahead) </fast> and <3> erm </3>

S1: <3> so you're </3> here with the idea of a presentation visual that's for the public (.) and we hand in a: a: written a:<4> written </4> e:r <un><5> xxxx</5></un>

S4: <4> yah </4>

S3: <4> sure </4>

S2: <5> great great </5>

SX-f: yah

S4: yah

S1: all right?

S4: great =

SX-f: = (erm) (.)

(VOICE: EDCon521: 238 - 252)

Example (1.1) is from an open and written form of "discourse completion task". Turn taking is one by one in conversations collected in this way, and speakers involved in this task have no choice to extend the conversations' topic. Moreover, all answers are offered with a second thought or with a revised version. While for speakers in example (1.2), interlocutors are much freer to add anything, and they would hesitate, repeat and even make grammatical mistakes while they are speaking. Comparing those two kinds of data, the former one lacks its authenticity and naturalness, though it is clearer and more specific in expression. In spite of that, this does not necessarily mean that discourse completion task is of little value. It has been used as a short cut to get the data that meet the researchers' requirement. As for the naturally occurring data, it is more valuable and trustworthy for research. However, it is more time-consuming, and moreover a lot of work needs to be done before finding the appropriate data. In order to get more natural and reliable data, this book will concentrate more on naturally occurring conversations which involve non-native speakers.

The classroom setting, especially the second language classroom, is a common wayto collect intercultural communication data. There are both merits and demerits in this kind of data. In the classroom setting, speakers' varied cultural backgrounds provide abundant intercultural communication sources. However, Cogo and Dewey (2012) also put that "talks in second language classrooms do not indeed constitute natural conversation". Obviously, a conversation in a typical classroom setting as mentioned by Cogo and Dewey (2012) is not convincing enough, since teachers may play the role of leading learners, and task-oriented conversations are unavoidable (Kasper, 2000; Block, 2003). What's more, in a second language classroom students may under go the pressure of having to perform in a better way. Therefore, more attention is paid to language forms instead of content, which makes the data a kind of performance rather than natural and spontaneous conversations (Cogo et al., 2012). A part of the data used in the following sections is from recording a language-learning group. Although we have already mentioned that classroom settings make conversations not as natural and spontaneous as naturally occurring conversations, some specific details of this language-learning group are worthy of our attention.

Generally speaking, second language learning class or foreign language learning class usually aims to improve learners' language skills systematically in all aspects, such as listening, speaking, reading and writing. Different from that, this language learning group is much more natural, and so will the source of recording. The aim of the class is to encourage everyone who takes part in it to speak freely, and questions related to culture or whatever aspects they may come across in daily life are welcomed at any time. Besides, there is no restriction on topics and no evaluation on performance. The volunteer is always ready to help if anyone has any questions. Therefore, the problems that matter in a class setting actually do not count in this case. The first part of data discussed in this book is mainly transcribed and collected from that group. Besides recordings from the language learning group, other sources of dataand daily conversations transcriptions are also important ways to collect data. Daily conversations among native speakers of English and non-native speakers from different cultures are involved. In addition, some ready-made corpus will be applied in the following discussion, such as VOICE, which consists of "naturally occurring, non-scripted face-to-face interaction in English as a lingua franca". Therefore, that part of data is also naturally occurring instead of task oriented.

In a word, the data we use in this study is mainly from naturally occurring conversations. In order to increase the variability of the data corpus, we try to collect data from different sources. Conversations between two or among three or more non-native interlocutors instead of monologues are the required data in this book. Great efforts have been devoted to collecting the data in order to ensure that the empirical data that we are dealing with is based on naturally occurring conversations. In the following discussion, more details of the data used in this study will be given.

### 1.3.2 Data Description

There are several sources of data that we will resort to in this book. On the one hand, most of the data is collected from live communication, which is quite demanding, and much commitment has been devoted to this work, such as recording, transcription, proofreading and revision and so on. On the other hand, a part of data is from online corpus, which has already been transcribed and revised, and thus no extra work is needed.

The recorded data is from a language-learning group in a public library in Albany, New York. No specific rules have been laid down for the group members of this language-learning group to obey. In this group, a native speaker is recruited as a volunteer, who functions as a guide or a director. A female senior plays this role in the group, and she is somehow a teacher or a friend to other non-native speakers. Other speakers in this group are all non-native speakers of English from all over the world. Most of them speak different first languages, and English thus is the second language for them to communicate with each other. Some of the non-native speakers are new to the language environment, others have stayed in America a little longer, while the rest may have been in America for years. Although the time that they stay in the US differs, what they have in common is that they are not as proficient as native speakers of English. Their English proficiency has been evaluated as advanced (comparing with other groups of non-native speakers who attend this project) before joining in that group (there are two other groups in which participants evaluated as preliminary or medium are suggested to join). At the beginning of each class, every attendant will briefly tell others about what he or she has been doing or anything interesting that they have come across during the previous week. While it starts with individual speaking, this is not necessarily a monologue, since anyone may cut in and ask questions or make comments at any time. There is no restriction on topics and no evaluation on performance. The volunteer, who is involved in the conversation as well, is always ready to help if anyone encounters any questions. The data in this book is mainly collected and transcribed from the communication recordings of this language-learning group. The data transcribed contains about 52,743 words, mainly from 11 pieces of recordings, which lasts about 7—8 hours in total.

Besides the recorded data, there are a lot of online corpusses available. To meet the requirement of this study, we choose VOICE as the source of online data after several rounds ofselection. VOICE is an online corpus in which all the data is from communication among speakers who use English as a lingua franca. As put in the corpus description, VOICE consists of "transcripts of naturally occurring, non-scripted face-to-face interactions in English as a lingua franca". All speakers involved in the interactions speak a wide variety of first languages, and have varied cultural backgrounds. The interactions cover all kinds of speech events, which have been classified into different categories according to different standards. In terms of domain, they are divided into the professional, educational and leisure one. As to the functions, both exchanging information and enacting social relationships are involved. With regard to participant roles and relationships, they are acquainted vs. unacquainted and symmetrical vs. asymmetrical. As for the speech event types, there are interviews, press conferences, service encounters, seminar discussions, working group discussions, workshop discussions, meetings, panels, question-answer-sessions, conversations and so on. Although all the data are about non-native speakers, what we mainly focus on will be interviews and conversations. This has to do with different features of various speech types, among which only interviews and conversations involve frequent and immediate interactions.

Those different sources of data are what the study is built on. The three basic requirements that the source of data should follow have been listed here: First, as a study on non-native speakers' communication, at least one non-native speaker should be involved. Second, it should be a dialogue instead of a monologue or report. Third, it should be communication that occur in immediate context. All the data that we select meet the requirements mentioned above. Three forms of pragmatic creativity have been found in our data: pragmatic creativity in grammatical forms, in lexical forms and by deviating collocation. Detailed analysis will be given in Chapter Four.

# Chapter Two  Literature Review

Creativity is not a new concept in academic research, especially in linguistics. For example, the topic "bilingual creativity" (Bolton et al., 2006) accounts for almost ten percent of the articles in *World Englishes*. While in 2007, a special issue of *Applied Linguistics* was published to show recent achievements on everyday creativity in language (Swann et al., 2007: 491). In addition, a collection of *Creativity in Language and Literature: The State of the Art* (Swann et al., 2011) came out as motivated by a series of seminars held at Open University in 2007, not to mention that quite a number of articles out there are not presented in a bunch. But what is creativity? How do linguists connect it with language? Do all studies related to creativity in language refer to the same thing? All these questions need to be answered first before we continue to discuss pragmatic creativity.

Nevertheless, not much consensus has been achieved on the notion of creativity. Some scholars take it as "a personal attribute, associated more with some domains than with others" (Burton, 2010: 494), which means that someone who is creative in a certain field is capable of providing more brilliant or original ideas; while others refer to it as "an intriguing human ability, with far-reaching importance to science and society" (Prabhakaran et al., 2014: 641). They all take practical issues into considerations when dealing with the concept. The root of western conception of creativity can be traced back to ancient Greek, which means "creating something completely new out of nothing through divine inspiration" (Burton, 2010: 494). Though its divinity has been doubted by the modern world, its core concept of creating something new has been inherited by lots of scholars, such as Rhodes (1961), Burton (2010), Prabhakaran and Green (2014), etc. Creativity, as put in Oxford English dictionary, is "the faculty of being creative, ability or power to create". From a writer's point of view, creativity is defined as the "bisociation of unrelated matrices" (Koestler, 1964: 35); taken as a cognitive capacity, creativity is "the ability to come up with new ideas that are surprising yet intelligible, and valuable in some way" (Boden, 2001: 95); linguistically, creativity is generally treated as the property of language users who not only reproduce, but also "recreate, refashion, and re-contextualize linguistic and cultural resources" (Swann et al., 2007: 491) in communication. In Swann and Maybin's opinion, the strategic way that language is used should be regarded as "creative" as well, which is also supported by a lot of scholars (Pennycook, 2007; Cogo, 2009; 2010; 2012; Cogo et al., 2012).

Although there are so many ready-made definitions for creativity, none of them fits well in our study here. Before we take a further step, some questions proposed at the beginning of this chapter should be answered first, for instance, whether context should be counted in or not and what related speakers' attribute is. With answers to those questions clear in mind, we can then go further with the development of creativity in linguistics and explore what pragmatic creativity refers to in this book. In this chapter, we will try to review previous studies of creativity and language from three different perspectives: rhetorical creativity, linguistic creativity and pragmatic creativity.

## 2.1 Reviews of Rhetorical Creativity

Analyses of creativity in language for rhetorical effects fall into two categories: creativity in literary language and non-literary language(Carter et al., 2004; Swann et al., 2007; Jones, 2010). Such a distinction is made roughly on the basis of data, which includes literature works and non-literary language. Thus, we will briefly look into how scholars deal with different kinds of data in this section. Since there is an imbalance of study between literary data and non-literary data, more attention will be paid to the study of non-literary language.

### 2.1.1 Creativity in Literary Language

The term "literary language" used here mainly refers to the language used in creative writing or literature works in comparison to the non-literary language that will be addressed in the following section. As for this kind of data, scholars mostly pay attention to the literary creativity, including figures of speech and styles.

On the one hand, rhetorical devices, such as metaphor, hyperbole, irony and repetition, are supposed to be components of creative writing. According to Pope (2005: 1), those "creative" words in pre-nineteenth century are always closely related to "artistic senses", such as parody, mimicry, imitation, revision and repetition and so on, all of which are regarded as "meaning-making" strategies (Tannen, 1989: 97; Pennycook, 2007: 579). "Creative writers" (Kim et al., 2012: 43) are even assumed to use metaphors more efficiently. Metaphor has always been taken as "a literary property" to offer a new perspective to "human experience" (Carter, 2004: 71). Mimicry, mimesis or "deliberate repetition of sameness", as Pennycook (2007: 586) puts it, is more than repetition but "modifies the original" (Fuchs, 2001: 5) and endows a new relationship between the new one and the original one in arts or discourse (Bhabha, 1985; Taussig, 1993).

On the other hand, although figures of speech are effective means to be creative, lots of studies on literary works have noticed a higher level of language use and style (Carter et al., 2004; Simpson et al., 2002; Rojas-Drummond et al., 2008). Scholars analyze literary stylistics of text by applying linguistic instruments, which are known as discourse stylistics (Simpson et al., 2002). Dynamics between literary works and their readers, literary and historical texts and fictional narrative are analyzed in terms of politeness theory, conversational analysis and speech act theory and so on (Pratt, 1977; Magnusson, 1999; Norrick, 2000).

Besides, phonology and phonaesthetics have been introduced to analyze creativity in literary works (Robbins, 2013), which benefits both disciplines significantly. However, there are still a lot to be done in the study of creativity of language. In the following section, we will briefly discuss the studies of creativity in non-literary language.

### 2.1.2 Creativity in Non-literary Language

Researchers have argued that there should be a broader research scope of the study of creativity instead of only sticking to the language of literary works or skills of creative writing (Cook, 1997; Crystal, 1998; Carter, 1999; 2004; Maybin et al., 2007). Norrick's discussion of "the poetics of conversation" brings non-literary language to the public's attention (Norrick, 2000: 452). Carter and McCarthy (2004: 62) hold the opinion that non-canonical texts that put emphasis on daily discourses will lead to "the breaking down of division between literary and non-literary language". Carter argues that "linguistic creativity is not simply a property to exceptional people but an exceptional property of all people" (Carter, 2004: 13). This is exactly one of the attributes of creativity in other fields. In *Language and Creativity: The Art of Everyday Talk*, Carter (2004) also provides several keywords to develop everyday creativity, such as "novelty" "genius" "originality" and so on. He also suggests that it is more possible that creativity will occur in non-institutionalized, familiar and informal social context. The reason is that risk for interpersonal communication is lowered in such kind of context. Therefore, creativity in non-literary language is more prone to occur. While in studying non-literary language, it is interesting that scholars lay their emphasis not only on general speakers but also on non-native speakers. In the following discussion, we would review studies related to different speakers separately.

Rhetorical creativity is not limited to literature, and it can also be found in non-literary language (Johnson, 1987; Lakoff et al., 1999; Gavins et al., 2003). A lot of studies have contributed to the former topic, either named as "the manipulation of linguistic form" (Maybin et al., 2007: 498) or "the poetic function of language" (Jakobson, 1960: 356). It indicates that "there is 'a focus on the message for its own sake'" (Swann, 2006: 10). This kind of manipulation or function in non-literary language partly refers to the figures of speech. It is known as words with "artistic sense" (Pope, 2005: 1), the same as that in literary works.

Tannen (1989) explores figures of speech in conversational poetic forms, such as repetition, while most studies conventionally focus on literary works at that time. Some scholars pay attention to non-literary language, not only to the verbal repetition, but also to other figures of speech in non-literary language. In studying the CANCODE (The Cambridge and Nottingham Corpus of

Discourse in English), Carter and McCarthy (2004: 63) have identified the key features in language such as "metaphor, simile, metonymy, idiom, slang expressions, proverbs and hyperbole" and so on. In applying those creative means, some may be used by speakers on purpose, while the rest may be used by interlocutors without noticing.

As one of the research areas in creativity of non-literary language, poetic creativity is frequently mentioned, in which figures of speech and other linguistic devices are employed in everyday conversations to achieve certain communicative goals.

Challenging the traditional conception that literariness is limited to literature, scholars broaden their research scope to non-literary language so as to explore how "everyday spoken discourse display literary properties" (Carter, 1999: 195). Besides the poetic creativity, linguists also attend to the creativity displayed in terms of register or speaking styles in non-literary language.

Register, as a kind of language form used for a specific purpose or in a particular social setting, is one of the indispensables. Halliday, McIntosh and Strevens (1964) have proposed that three aspects are associated with register: field, mode and tenor. The whole event, function of the text in the event, type of role interaction as well as their social relation are included. Speakers usually use different language styles, sometimes called register; those vary when topics, occasions or media change (Atchison, 1999). In non-literary language, register helps people go smoothly with their talk, which is also taken as creativity. Cohesion of text, as Halliday and Hasan (1976: 23) put it, can be "usefully supplemented by that of register". Besides, deliberate overlapping of different registers may also bring certain unexpected communicative effect. For example, on informal occasions, using some formal words or expressions may make audience burst into laughter.

Roach (2001) puts forward that various registers that we are using are called code. Code mixing is widely used in daily communication or non-literary language. North (2007: 551) has come up with the opinion that it is not only cohesion that composes the group but also the boundaries they build that mark others outside. When it comes to register, people in particular a situation or for a specific purpose can use it to create and even to maintain the group so as to distinguish the insiders from the outsiders.

Different speaking styles are also very common in non-literary language, such as "style shifting, code-switching and crossing" (Maybin et al., 2007: 499) and so on. Style shifting in public or individual language may show language attitudes (Hernández-Campoy et al., 2013), since different language expressions used in advertisements or brand names may show different tastes (Piller, 2011). Code switching may help construct identity (John et al., 2014), especially in multilingual settings (Mensah et al., 2013). Language crossing, as a form of code switching, could affect ideology in the area (Rampton, 2005). Zawada holds the opinion that choosing from different formulaic forms or expressions of greeting may"affect the register of the discourse" (2006: 249). To some degree, style or register influences discourse in an all-around way.

Stylistics in non-literary language is not limited to the text, since contexts, speakers' identities and other necessary conditions that build a conversation will constitute its own stylistics, which displays language creativity. As for register, code and speaking style are creative aspects of language use in non-literary language, through which different communicative effects are created and diverse communicative purposes are achieved.

## 2.2 Reviews of Linguistic Creativity

Since we have had a brief discussion on rhetorical creativity both in literary and non-literary language, and before we take a further step to pragmatic creativity, there is an important issue that we should chew over: how is creativity understood in linguistics? It is the key issue in the following discussion.

In studies of linguistic creativity, "formal aspects of language in use" (Jones, 2010: 467) or creativity in linguistic approach (Cook, 2000) has been emphasized, which deals with the relation between language forms and how they are organized to form sentences or texts so as to express meanings. It is in a systematic sense. On the other hand, creativity is also related to discourse, in which language is used in social context with certain communicative purposes, such as studies of non-native speakers' communication mentioned above. The former one is what we are going to discuss in this section. Besides, there is also another approach in studies of creativity in language called "creative process" (Tin, 2011), such as "ordered" "chaotic thinking" (Finke, 1996) and so on, which is beyond our concern. Creativity has been taken as a "graded phenomenon" which manifests "in all domains of language" (Zawada, 2006: 235), and it is suggested that we should study "the entire system" (Ward et al., 1997: 18) so as to have a comprehensive view of the relationship between creativity and language. In the following section, we will go through previous studies of linguistic creativity, which focus on studies of language in use.

Linguistic creativity, which has been discussed for quite a long time in linguistic field, has gained a lot of understandings according to different scholars. In applied linguistics, creativity of language forms "patterns of formal features" and "linguistic idiosyncracies of particular texts" (Cook, 1998: 205), in which language play is one of the most important media (Cook, 2000: 1). From the cognitive perspective, linguistic creativity could be understood in two ways: the primary one is an activity to create new meanings by the speaker and recreated by the hearer, while the secondary is taken as a product of language (Zawada, 2006: 235). Zawada's research covers language forms ranging from lexical level, syntactic level to discourse level. Emphasis on forms or patterns is the main focus in linguistic creativity.

Hudson (2000: 10) has pointed out that creativity of language is due to its recursion and openness, which could be understood as generative creativity and lexical creativity respectively. The former mainly refers to the use of existing components to form new expressions or sentences, while the latter discusses creativity at the lexical level such as creating a new word. We will adopt that classification and discuss the categories in the following sections.

### 2.2.1 Generative Creativity

In 1957, a psychologist B. F. Skinner published a book *Verbal Behavior*, in which he describes what is traditionally called linguistics. In his book, Skinner acknowledges that "generalized pattern imposed on the specific acts as they occur" (1957: 512), which is later called "syntactic structure" by Chomsky (1964a: 575), can only be "inferred by the final result of their activity" (Skinner, 1957: 509). In opposition to Skinner's claims, Chomsky (1964a: 578) argues that if we just limit language study to a step called "generalization" then lots of studies will be mysteries, and if the absent language is like mimicking and memorization, then basically we exclude creativity. It is Chomsky who later brings creativity into the center of linguists' attention (Den Ouden,

1975; Sampson, 1979; 1980; Fred, 1984).

Chomsky proposes that when a speaker produces new sentences in communication, his hearer usually could get it immediately; therefore, he puts forward that,

> Once we have mastered a language, the class of sentences with which we can operate fluently and without difficulty or hesitation is so vast that for all practical purposes . . . we may regard it as infinite.
>
> (Chomsky, 1964b: 7)

The ability of producing infinite expressions and sentences by finite language sources is originally understood by Chomsky as mastering a grammar, a form of generative and transformational alternatives. In Chomsky's point of view, being generative in language is equal to being creative in choosing or generating new expressions, and "a generative grammar must be a system of rules that can iterate to generate an indefinitely large number of structures" (Chomsky, 1965: 15 – 16). His understanding of creativity falls within the range of "recursive property to the syntactic component" (Chomsky, 1972: 155). That kind of ability is parallel with what Chomsky calls "creative aspect of language use" (Chomsky, 1964b: 8; Den Ouden, 1975: 12). In Chomsky's (1972: 11) point of view, a sentence with the recursive property assigned refers to "an indefinite number of expressions which are new to" his "experience" (1972: 100) which language users speak and understand. The word "generate" equals to his opinion that human beings could be creative in language. Chomsky (1972: 103) holds that mechanism of such kind of creativity can be described. While for "creative aspect of language use", it refers to human ability to form a statement so as to express their thought and respond (Chomsky, 1966: 4). This falls into "textual creativity", which does not belong to creativity in the narrow sense (Kecskes, 2003: 136). The connection between these two kinds of creativity is "form" and "character" (Chomsky, 1966: 27). The former provides "the means" (Chomsky, 1974: 28) for the latter; however, it also should be noted that a lot of linguists haven't made a clear distinction between those two concepts.

Following Chomsky's study, many scholars continue with the topic that generative production of language or linguistic productivity is creativity in language. Fred (1984: 87) puts forward that language users show speakers' "Cartesian" creativity by using some new expressions that are not determined by context (Chomsky, 1966: 13), which is known as the creativity of ordinary language use (Fred, 1984: 114). Carter (2004: 78) argues that Chomsky's notion of creativity here generally refers to speaker's ability to master the underlying language system. Novelty in producing language matches with Chomsky's notion of linguistic creativity, and North (2007: 539) also points out that linguistic creativity is to combine things already in existence in a new way instead of creating something out of nothing. This is especially correspondent with language learners' learning process. When communicating with others, speakers need to make use of what they have in mind, so as to construct new meanings, reanalyze and combine the old forms to form new ones (Tin, 2011: 219). Linguistic creativity in Chomsky's opinion is also favored by lots of applied linguists, in a sense that a competent language user could both construct and understand an infinite number of new expressions or utterances in both written and spoken forms (Bell, 2012: 191).

Besides human beings' ability to create, scholars also devote themselves to the wide research of generative creativity in language. One of the directions is the poetic creativity in language, which is also covered in Chomsky's "creative aspect oflanguage use", including applying figures of speech. Carter (2004) defines two different processes of linguistic creativity: pattern forming and pattern re-forming. Pattern forming refers to the use of existing language resources to create certain effect, such as repetition, parallel, alliteration etc., especially in context that those will generally not appear. Pattern reforming includes using pun, new words, hyperbole, metaphor, idioms etc., and perfecting all those figures of speech to achieve linguistic creativity. In this way, rules and conventions are broken so that concepts will be specialized. In short, speakers generate new meanings by making use of existing language resources. Patrick (2008) proposes that the main function of natural language is to express one's idea, including a new one. The new idea can always be compared with the old one, which is achieved through simile. Rhetoric of the same kind can always attract the hearers' attention and inspire their imagination. Su Xiaoyu (1999) analyzes literary metaphors in computer language and summarizes features of linguistic creativity as metonymy, misspelling, double capital letters, acronym, ambiguity, humor and so on. Shi Yan (2008) goes specifically from the view of figures of speech, including onomatopoeia, homophonic, parody, metonymy, metaphor and so on. In his opinion, "rhetoric is both synchronic and diachronic", and "it is not only the phenomenon of language deviation but also meaning changing could be taken as a mechanism of linguistic creativity" (2008: 87).

While some scholars are studying how people make new sentences, others are working on the generative mechanism of language, which has been used as L2 (second language) or lingua franca, so as to promote language education (Kramsch, 2007; Carter, 2007; Cogo, 2009; 2010). Liu Chendan (2012: 31) proposes that, syntactically speaking, "speakers should produce all kinds of language structures if they want to use finite linguistic units to express infinite information". In addition, he also divides structural boundary movement into reasonable and unreasonable ones. The former refers to rules obeyed when the boundaries of structures are re-assigned; otherwise, it is unreasonable (Liu, 2012: 31). Therefore, from the deep structure, we can see that the same sentence can produce different meanings once the boundary changes, and it is the boundary that leads to linguistic creativity.

In regards to generative creativity, the key concern of linguists is how people can express infinite meanings with finite words and grammatical rules. Ways to achieve that aim vary from "recursive structure" advocated by Chomsky and his followers to different figures of speech in expressing or constructing new meanings within limited sources.

### 2.2.2 Lexical Creativity

#### 2.2.2.1 Analogy vs. Metaphor

The study of lexical creativity is always connected with word formation as well as metaphor, metonymy, loan words, acronyms, clippings and blends and so on (Lipka, 1994; 2002; 2007). Gay (1980) used to compare two models of linguistic creativity, which are analogy and metaphor. He (1980: 312) also holds the opinion that Saussure's study of linguistic creativity is mainly on the lexical and syntactic level, which takes "analogy innovation" as creativity and "looks at individual words standing in opposition and examines unrealized possibilities in grammar". Therefore, analogical creativity is achieved through grammatically modifying existing vocabularies. For example, the noun "priority" could lead to a new verb according to the rule that transforms "authority" into "authorize". Another model mentioned by Gay (1980: 312) is that at the syntactic and semantic level, which Ricoeur has paid much attention to. It is about linear combination of vocabularies and semantic possibilities of unfulfilled forms. For Ricoeur, the core of linguistic creativity is how metaphor expands meanings of a polyseme synchronically, and numbers of polysemes diachronically (Gay, 1980: 311). As a comprehensive model of linguistic creativity, Gay (1980: 314) insists that there are necessity and deficiency in both models. The necessity lies in that both models are based on linguistic facts, while the deficiency is that both lack the creative types mentioned in the other. Despite the fact that it has covered quite a wide range of studies of language creativity, the discussion based on an utterance or discourse level has not yet been mentioned.

### 2.2.2.2 Productivity vs. Creativity

Bauer (1983: 63), following Lyons, defines productivity as "rule-governed innovation" while creativity as "rule changing". He (1988: 62) also points out that productivity of vocabulary is "some measurement of generalization", and this "productivity" is considered as a "cline" (Bauer, 1988: 57). This is also supported by Gupta (1992: 11), who distinguishes productivity from creativity and illustrates the differences by the following figure:

**Table 1. More productive word-formation rules vs. less productive word-formation strategies**

| Word-Formation Rules | Word-Creation Strategies |
|---|---|
| ← | → |
| Productive | Unproductive |
| Regular | Irregular |
| Predictive | Unpredictive |
| e.g. derivation and compounding | e.g. clipping and blending |

The huge differences between word-formation rules and word-creation strategies only lead the former to the scope of linguistic creativity study. Therefore, to clarify differences between the two aspects is the premise to define the scope of linguistic creativity.

#### 2.2.2.3 Explanatory vs. Predictive

Veale Tony and others (2006: 1) who pay special attention to the creative lexical forms, introduce lexical creativity from the perspective of lexicology. They also divide lexical creativity into two types: explanatory and predictive. Explanatory creativity analyzes new vocabulary's structure, while predictive creativity makes use of the relation between vocabulary and its potential corresponding encyclopedic usage that vocabulary may denote. In their study, both word forms and meanings are taken as ways to be creative in communication. Lipka (2007: 6) has pointed out that most articles in lexical creativity focus on "patterns and categories" of word formation, and "blends are specifically treated". However, in the traditional study of lexical creativity, lexicons in discourse and utterances are ignored, and only a few studies are related as mentioned at the beginning of this section.

#### 2.2.2.4 Meaning vs. Form

Studies of lexical creativity at home cover creative meanings and forms of vocabulary as well. With the development of technology, languages, especially Internet language, catch linguists' eye. Tang Meiying (2010) discusses the motivation and improper orientation of Internet language. The Internet language that she refers to includes creation of vocabulary both in meanings and forms. Huang Yeping and Hou Pan (2012: 238) also made some investigations into Internet language. They believe that it is "a new type of language style" with "unique cultural attribute", and its "humor, richness and fashion cater today's aesthetic needs and reflect people's aesthetic psychology". The study of Internet language, which is non-ideal but actual, is a new variant in linguistic creativity.

Liu Chendan (2012) points out that boundary movement is a motivation for linguistic creativity, and he also introduces polysemy from the view of implicit boundary movement. In his opinion, "meaning change does not accomplish at one stroke but as a shift from space domain to space-and-time domain, then to simple time domain, and finally to personal will domain, and after that it will be functionalizedand grammaticalized" (2012: 32). In Liu's (2012) point of view, polysemy is the result of both diachronic and synchronic phenomenon; therefore, it should be the object of study in linguistic creativity instead of hapax legomena mentioned by other scholars as below.

#### 2.2.2.5 Hapax Legomena

Bauer (1988: 65) mentioned that "hapax legomena" in individual's vocabulary and words that "even more frequently never come within the scrutiny of the professional linguist or grammarian" do not fall into linguists' or grammarians' scope of study. He holds that linguists and grammarians should focus on language study as a social product at the lexical and grammatical level. However, such kind of restriction excludes words that lie outside normative language system but still will appear in utterances. Zawada (2005: 55) supports that linguists who pay attention to speaker's abilities to create new expressions should not miss hapax legomena. The problem is that it is not easy to collect data such as "hapax legomena", and therefore, it may not be applied to linguistic study. However, as more and more corpusses appear, the possibility of "capturing at least some of these instances of novel expressions" increases a great deal (Zawada, 2005: 55). Besides, "excluding 'non-ideal' but actual linguistic facts from theoretical study may lower credibility of theoretical explanation" (Liu et al., 2005: 32). Therefore, in linguistic study, attentions should be paid not only to those ideal linguistic facts, but also to actual ones without neglecting "non-ideal" ones. Except those "one-time word", quite a lot of other studies explore lexical creativity in practical use from different angles. On the one hand, more kinds of lexical creativity are under study, such as political correctness (Fisher, 2007), nonce word formation (Hohenhaus, 2007). On the other hand, lexical creativity is related to specific linguistic environment. For example, Kuiper (2007) studies lexical creativity in inter-semiotic environment, and Lehrer (2007) studies newspaper and magazine headings, advertisements and new product names, while Lopez Rua (2007) exploits the issue in electronic communication and so on.

#### 2.2.2.6 Errors vs. Creativity

Scholars both at home and abroad focus on lexical creativity in meaning and forms. Most studies go through lexical creativity in communication among native speakers; however, for non-native speakers, lexical creativity offers a complete different view.

Generally speaking, there are two aspects concerned with lexical studies relate to non-native speakers. As mentioned above, lexical borrowing, loan words by translation, coinage, acronyms, clipping, ellipsis (Hashim et al., 2012; 2013) and others are means for general speakers in both literary works and non-literary language to be creative. Besides, modes of address and reference, semantic shift as well as hybridization are also considered as non-native features of lexicon in Thai English fiction (Hashim et al., 2012; 2013). On the other hand, errors made by non-native speakers are sometimes viewed as a kind of creativity as well (Yang et al., 2001). Generally speaking, a word created by non-native speakers is taken as a lexical error. However, as Carter (2007: 605) proposes that the line between creative and error doesn't change with the speaker. For non-native speakers, errors are creative coinages, in some sense. It is proposed that two types of errors at the lexical or syntactical level should be distinguished from each other. One is the inappropriate use of words, while the other is the creation of new word forms, such as hapax legomena mentioned above.

While at the pragmatic level, there is another kind of creativity in non-native speakers' language use. Carter (2007) mentions in his paper that a "native-speaker voice" is very important for a second language learner. For non-native speakers, selecting a word that is preferred by native speakers could be considered as a kind of creativity. That is to say, speaking in a native-like way is a kind of creativity for non-native speakers, while this is based on the selection of native-like words and expressions. Since the details about studies of creativity in non-native speakers' communication have been discussed in the previous section, we will not go any further.

## 2.3 Reviews of Pragmatic Creativity

Studies of creativity in language are mainly probed from the linguistic perspective, in which generative and lexical creativity are of the primary concern. Realization of linguistic creativity requires social convention, while from the pragmatic perspective, its fulfillment calls for the acceptance of both the speaker and hearer. Once a hearer accepts and understands the specific utterance or discourse, and then responds as the speaker's wish, the process of creativity is fulfilled. Jones (2010) also puts it as discourse and creativity. In this book, we will introduce a new notion, namely pragmatic creativity, to separate it from linguistic creativity. Although linguistic creativity has caught many linguistic scholars' attention, the research on creativity in language from the pragmatic perspective has also aroused many scholars' interest (Gerrig et al., 1988; Prevignano et al., 2003; Maybin et al., 2007; Zawada, 2006; Jones, 2010; Tsakona, 2012). In their opinions, pragmatic factor is one of the indispensible elements in language creativity. In this section, we will first review the previous studies of language creativity from the pragmatic perspective, and then introduce the concept of pragmatic creativity proposed by other scholars briefly as a counterpart of linguistic creativity.

### 2.3.1 Creativity Involving Pragmatic Factors

At the beginning of the previous section, we claim that it is Chomsky who brings creativity into the center of linguists' attention. Scholars in this field devote themselves to the study of creativity from various aspects; however, as Chomsky pays his attention solely to the generative aspect of linguistic creativity, most scholars following him also look into linguistic creativity at the syntactic and semantic level. In spite of that, still some researches focus on creativity in language from the pragmatic perspective, which is about non-literary language in context. The study of creativity in language adopts sources from both literary and non-literary language; however, one thing that we should make clear before going further is that the study of creativity in non-literary language does not necessarily mean to study creativity in language at the pragmatic level.

In researches of creativity in language, "non-native speaker" is usually taken as a marked feature compared with "native speaker". Creativity in communication among native speakers is usually taken as creativity in general. In the following section, we will look into previous studies of creativity from the pragmatic perspective concerned with both native and non-native speakers.

#### 2.3.1.1 Native Speakers' Creativity from the Pragmatic Perspective

Even in terms of creativity at the pragmatic level, there are different perspectives. Gerrig and Gibbs (1988) discuss the motivations of linguistic creativity, believing that pragmatic factors are involved. Zawada (2006) concludes the factors as follows: first of all, linguistic creativity can transmit information directly to the hearer; secondly, in persuasive language, creative utterance can leave the hearer a deeper impression; finally, linguistic creativity may rise due to politeness or social pressure under certain tough circumstances. In addition, Gerrig and Gibbs make a simple distinction between linguistic productivity and linguistic creativity. They hold the opinion that the former one suggests "speakers construct utterances through combination of conventional words accessed from the mental dictionary" (1988: 13). In their opinion, "when speakers produce lexical innovations, metaphor, or indirect speech acts, there is no one-to-one mapping between their intended meaning and words in the lexicon" (Gerrig et al., 1988: 13). Creativity here is similar to the linguistic way, in which more emphasis is put on the meaning of utterance.

For language creativity from the pragmatic perspective, not only forms or meanings at the lexical, semantic or syntactic level are under study, but also its usage in discourse catches the scholars' attention. Jones (2010) proposes that when discussing discourse and creativity we should pay attention to the "value". In his opinion, "a concern with value is absolutely central — not in the sense of aesthetic value — but in the sense of pragmatic value". The pragmatic value here is not limited to the form and meaning of language, but how it "actually help us to accomplish things in the material world and in our relationships with others" (Jones, 2010: 471). In his point of view, creativity at the discourse level can both "take actions in the world" and exert constraints over the actions (Jones, 2010: 473). Function of creativity is one of the aspects discussed by linguists who study creativity at the pragmatic level (Maybin et al., 2007; Tsakona, 2012).

Carter and McCarthy (2004) also acknowledge that there are different purposes or functions through using poetic or artistic creativity in everyday speech:

> "The purpose of creative language . . . include: offering some new way of seeing the content of the message; making humorous remarks; underlining what is communicated; expressing a particular attitude, including negative and adversarial attitude; making the speaker's identity more manifest; playing with language form to entertain others; ending one bit of talk and starting another; or simply oiling the wheels of the conversation."
>
> (Carter et al., 2004: 64)

There are plenty of supporting evidences in non-literary language with purposes mentioned above. For example, the following is a classic conversational extract from Maybin and Swann (2007), in which Joan Swann is one of the participants when the family were having a picnic and feeding the pigeons:

(2.1) A: He might look scruffy but he's seen off that one over there.

B: Obviously a thug amongst pigeons.

C: Al Capigeon.

D: The godfather.

(Laughter overlaps C&D)

(Maybin et al., 2007: 506)

In the above conversation, B compares one of the pigeons to a thug, and C manipulates the linguistic form through "a blend of pigeon and Al Capone" (Maybin et al., 2007: 506), while D uses a pun to denote a pigeon both as a thug and an Al Capigeon. It is the common knowledge for them that Al Capone is the godfather of a Chicago gangster, and in the famous movie *The Godfather*, the hero is the leader of the gangster. Apparently here the interlocutors are all aware of the humor in this conversation. Therefore, everyone laughs. In this case, all linguistic devices help to achieve the humorous effects.

While in communication where only native speakers are involved, theyshare more common ground, especially in social and cultural aspect, therefore, strategies, such as using figures of speech, idioms and formulaic expressions, will be applied during their communication (Su, 1999; Carter, 2004; Shi, 2008; Patrick, 2008; Kecskes, 2013). In addition, North (2007: 547) mentions that in native speakers' communication, "innuendo, a form of showing collaborative construction", is used at a high frequency. Such kind of "collaborative construction" is based on the common ground shared by native speakers. In the case, the hearer is forced to look for a reasonable explanation for the irrelevant message transmitted by the speaker, in which the ambiguity existing in utterance is implicitly implied. Take the following case as an example:

(2.2) Marisol: I am just . . . curious.

Opal: *So was the cat*. We all know what happened to him.

(*Devious Maid*, Season II, Episode 6)

Example (2.2) is a piece of conversation between a maid Opal and her potential hostess Marisol. Marisol is trying to dig out some secret of her fiancé, while Opal tries very hard to hide it. In their conversation, an idiom that "curiosity kills the cat" is applied.

According to this idiom and background information of their conversation, we can deduce that the cat died because of being curious, and Marisol says she is curious, so bad things may happen to Marisol if she continues to be so curious. Based on their common knowledge of this idiom, they both know what Opal implies in this conversation, which makes the utterance a warning as well as a threat.

Tsakona (2012) uses the case of Greek parliamentary discourse to discuss linguistic creativity and institutional design, in which she (Tsakona, 2012: 94 – 95) suggests that one function of linguistic creativity is to inspire audience' potential emotional connection by using metaphor in political discourse, which encourages the audience to think about political affairs in a new way instead of being limited to the institutional system. In her research, she notices that figures of speech, such as metaphor, hyperbole, parallelism, repetition, and creative language like idioms can be found in the speaker's utterance, which is used to defend his/her own innocence and break his/her competitor's lie. As mentioned in section 2.1, rhetoric creativity can be found in both literary works and non-literary language. However, when we discuss figures of speech in the previous section, the main point is that those linguistic devices are applied to create new language forms or a new way of presenting meaning. While at pragmatic level as we have mentioned at the beginning, context turns out to be an indispensible factor. Maybin and Swann (2007: 501) have also pointed out "the function of creativity — for example, building solidarity and friendly relations — also points to the potential of a more dynamic model, in which creativity is both contextualized and contextualizing".

When studying creativity from the pragmatic perspective, the view that context can be seen as the background of the text is against what has been mentioned by Duranti, Goodwin (1992) and North (2007). In their opinion, context is more a "collaborative construction accomplished through the text" (North, 2007: 345). This can be traced back to Goffman who also argues that it is interlocutors who cooperate with each other so as to find out how "the ongoing world supports this fitting" (1974: 247). Based on the context and interlocutors' mutual cooperation, certain communicative effect, such as humor (North, 2007), is achieved. Communicative effect is one of the functions that creativity at the pragmatic level intends to achieve as well.

There are some scholars who devote themselves to the study of creativity at the pragmatic level. It is noticed that utterance or discourse is taken as the carrier, while context is the essential condition. Even though forms and meanings are mentioned as well, the function of utterance is the most significant point at this level. One thing that we should notice is that the function of creativity from the pragmatic perspective fulfilled is in a communicative sense instead of Jakobson's "poetic" sense (Maybin et al., 2007: 514). Poetic creativity appears both in literary works and non-literary language, and when scholars are devoting themselves to the study of creativity, language itself is the key focus. However, while scholars are studying the communicative effect of utterance, more attention is paid to how utterance works in the context. Therefore, we consider this kind of creativity as pragmatic creativity in order to distinguish it from linguistic creativity. In the following discussion, we will discuss how other scholars understand the term "pragmatic creativity" in details.

#### 2.3.1.2 Non-native Speakers' Creativity from the Pragmatic Perspective

Maybin and Swann (2007: 497) argue that applied linguists

view creativity not only as "a property of especially skilled and gifted language users", which are known as literature authors, but also as an ability to produce expressions in non-literary language for each individual. When it comes to the distinction of native speakers and non-native speakers, we can also say that creativity is not only a property of native speakers, but also of non-native speakers.

According to Bloomfield (1933: 43), a native speaker of a language is someone who speaks in his native language, which makes "later-learned language" (Cook, 1999) skip the range of a native one by definition. On the contrary, a non-native speaker is someone who speaks in a "later-learned language", in other words, a second language or a foreign language. Such a speaker is supposed to be a "defective communicator" (Firth et al., 1997: 292), for he or she may not be adequate in fluency or equipped with sufficient social and cultural background information. In this section, we will look into the studies related to non-native speakers. Most studies mentioned above are about language creativity in native speakers' communication, and quite a number of studies also show solicitude for language creativity among non-native speakers. Therefore, emphasis will be put on studies of non-native speakers' language creativity in the following discussion.

Following the flourishing trend in studying creativity in general, scholars also show their interest in studying creativity in non-native speakers' communication. Although the phrase that we use is "non-native speaker", it covers quite a large number of people. Most scholars devote themselves to studying L2 learners (Lantolf, 1997; Carter, 1999; 2004; 2007; Bell, 2012), some focus on foreign language learning (Roh, 2001; Pitzl, 2009; Klimpfinger, 2009; Ander et al., 2010; Hamid et al., 2013), and others spare their efforts to study the use of lingua franca

(Huttner, 2009; Cogo, 2009; 2010). Lopez (2007) suggested that creativity varies when cultural groups and social contexts change. Therefore, we hold the opinion that creativity in non-native speakers' communication may differ from those in native speakers'. In this section, studies of non-native speakers' creativity in communication will be involved.

Communication is the general goal for non-native speakers to learn a second or foreign language. And the creativity occurring in communication via a second or foreign language shows a big difference from those in acquisition. In second language or foreign language acquisition, creativity helps acquire vocabulary and grammar of a certain language. While in communication, the main purpose is to convey the speakers' intention, and thus the grammatical correctness is a secondary concern.

In non-native speakers' communication, lingua franca always does its job. Lingua franca is a language used by non-native speakers whose first languages are different from others'. For people who are from different countries and speak different mother tongues, lingua franca is the most important media for them to communicate with each other. For example, English is used as a lingua franca in many European countries. Lexical creativity, such as French vocabularies combined with English, semantic shift or extensions, can be found when English is used as a lingua franca in France (Vettorel et al., 2013). In America, a country described as a "melting pot" or "salad bowl", English is also the most significant lingua franca, as well as the world's lingua franca. Except English, French (Low et al., 2009) and other languages sometimes function as a lingua franca as well. Therefore, lingua franca plays a role of vital importance in communication involving interlocutors who speak different first languages.

When lingua franca is applied in communication, some problems or "non-understandings" (Cogo et al., 2012) may occur for various reasons. In order to solve those problems and ensure successful communication, speakers whospeak different first languages have to be flexible and creative in communication. It is during this process that language creativity appears to facilitate the non-native speakers' communication. Relevant studies have shown how non-native speakers are creative in communication so as to avoid such problems or non-understanding.

In communication among native speakers, interlocutors share more common ground especially in social and cultural aspect. While in communication among non-native speakers, due to the lack of such kind of common ground, language creativity is different because of various linguistic backgrounds. In previous sections, scholars have noticed that in native speakers' communication, figures of speech are often applied. However, figures of speech, such as puns, used in communication may "derail the conversation" (Sherzer, 2002: 32 - 33). Therefore, in order to avoid misunderstandings in conversations, instead of applying complex phrases, idioms, proverbs, etc., non-native speakers would choose a more explicit way to convey what they intend to. Besides, idiomatic use cannot be mapped onto non-native speakers in ELF communication (Pitzl, 2010), because pragmatics concerned in communication is almost equal to semantics (Kecskes, 2013a) for speakers of lower language proficiency.

Lacking shared knowledge is always supposed to be another reason that prevents non-native speakers from successful communication. However, recent studies show that it is not always the case, and moreover, cultural differences in understanding lingua franca are often overlooked (Mauranen, 2009; Kaur, 2011; Cogo, 2012). People from globalized societies have used

English as a lingua franca, and cultural differences are tolerated (Kaur, 2011). Scholars hold the opinion that a different social and cultural background does not necessarily lead to communicative failure, and adopting some strategies creatively can make up for such deficiency. In addition, it is also suggested that there are fewer problems and more flexibility in ELF communication than one might assume (Cogo, 2009). Jones (2010: 472) supportsthat using language creatively is related to the "strategic way that language is used", and that creative product in language communication is supposed to be a "new way of dealing with" both linguistic situations and social relationships instead of a "linguistic product". Cogo (2010) and Dewey (2012) hold the opinion that "negotiation of meaning" and "supporting meaning-making process" construct communication when applying English as a lingua franca. Pragmatic accommodation or accommodation strategies is viewed as the key to successful ELF communication, which is realized through different convergence strategies, such as repetition, code-switching and so on, and all those strategies have various functions in communication (Cogo, 2007; 2009). Cogo and Dewey (2012) also summarize the strategies adopted by ELF speakers in both initiating negotiation and during negotiation. In the former, indicators in communication are supposed to be the strategy. Several indicators are mentioned, such as echo, explicit statement of non-understanding, no verbal response, inappropriate response and so on (Cogo et al., 2012: 118 - 119). While for the latter, repetition strategy, pre-empting strategy, repetition with elaboration in the form of non-verbal strategy and others also appear in Cogo and Dewey's extract examples. In the process of meaning making, strategies such as back channels, simultaneous talk, short response overlaps, completion overlaps, utterance completion, are mentioned (Cogo et al., 2012: 138). In addition to strategies, another interesting phenomenon also arouses the scholars' interest. For non-native speakers, there are two important issues. One is correctness and the other is effectiveness. In the previous section, we have briefly described the issue of language acquisition, which gives more attention to correctness. Hulmbauer (2010) discusses the overlap of correctness and communicative effectiveness. She looks into the relationship between some incorrect forms and their effects in ELF communication, and points out incorrect expressions or ways of speaking can be "alternative and creative ways of making meaning in intercultural communication" (Hulmbauer, 2010: 324).

Besides the opinion that lingua franca can be used in a creative way to forestall unsuccessful communication between interlocutors with various mother tongues, there is also another voice on what creativity is in non-native speakers' communication. Non-native speakers' expressions in communication are usually of "unnatural" characteristic from a native speaker's perspective, due to "imperfect phraseology" instead of "inadequate conceptual awareness" (Kecskes, 2013a: 119). Expressions with native-like selection are one of the means for non-native speakers to be creative in communication. Native-like selection refers to the ability of native speaker to express his meaning with grammatically correct and native-like expressions (Pawley et al., 1983: 191). It is often the case that non-native speakers express grammatically perfect sentences, but they are not in the way that native speakers will do. In every language, lots of ready-made constructions, such as phrases, sentence structures or word sequences, are usually more expressive than the combination of its components. However, speakers with a lingua franca usually have no idea about those ready-made expressions in actual communication, or how flexible they could be combined in utterances, which can help speakers convey their intention in a more efficient way or with particular communicative goals (Kecskes, 2013a: 119). Such "artfully mixing formulaic" or "prefabricated units" together with newly generated items, which are used to transmit non-native speaker's intention in communication, are creative in language (Van Lancker et al., 2004; Kecskes, 2013a). This kind of formulaic expressions or formulaic language in Kecskes' view is a reflection of social and cultural aspects instead of mere language structures, which is also known as preferred ways of communication for native speakers of a certain language. Let's take a look at the following two examples:

(2.3) A: Sorry.

B: You are fine. / It's ok.

(2.4) A: Sorry.

B: Nothing, nothing.

Both examples happen on the bus when speaker A steps on B's foot by accident. In example (2.3), B is a local, and his response is appropriate in that situation. While B in example (2.4) is a female non-native speaker from China, the natural response from B doesn't indicate that her English is not good enough to say "it's ok", but under the influence of her first language, literal translation turns out to be inevitable since she has only been in America for a few days. Therefore, as indicated by Kecskes (2013a), using formulaic language in a proper way turns out to be one of the conditions for language creativity. In Kecskes' opinion, such kind of expressions is the interaction among "grammatical rules, lexical choice, functional adequacy, situational appropriateness, stylistic preference, and norms of use" (2013a: 107). Therefore, in this way, a non-native speaker is creative when he applies native speakers' preferred way of expressing. For instance, in example (2.4), if the Chinese speaker B speaks in a way that B in example (2.3) does, and then she can be called as creative. However, in this book, native-like selection, such as example (2.3), is not what we pay attention to, and our attention will be focused on cases as example (2.4).

In this section, we have discussed the studies of non-native speakers' creativity in communication. When communicating with a lingua franca, misunderstandings or even unsuccessful communication will occur, which requires non-native speakers to be creative. In addition, the previous studies indicate that non-native speakers can be creative in communication in two ways. On the one hand, strategic ways of communication make non-native speakers creative in communication, since those ways help speakers avoid or forestall communicative failures. On the other hand, for non-native speakers, to be native-like in linguistic choices can be called as creative as well in some scholars' opinion. Through combining prefabricated expressionswith novel items in communication, non-native speakers speak in a native way. Vega-Moreno (2007: 217) suggests that successful communication depends on speakers' ability to "strike a balance between creativity and convention". For non-native speakers or in intercultural communication, successful communication also depends on the balance between creativity and convention. In this sense, non-native speakers' creativity should still be taken into account, otherwise, misunderstandings or non-understandings will be unavoidable.

### 2.3.2 Pragmatic Creativity

Based on a detailed review on linguistic creativity, this section will discuss what is pragmatic creativity and how it is differentiated from linguistic creativity.

In linguistic creativity studies, context is more often than not taken into consideration. Studies on creativity in the pragmatic sense have not always been separated from those in the linguistic sense. Not many scholars devote themselves to that differentiation, but luckily there is a trend that they start to pay attention to it. Creativity is considered to be "the basic process of language use", and from the externalist view, it is also "a violation of norms" (De Beaugrande, 1978: 2). Taking pragmatics into consideration, Gumperz (Prevignano et al., 2003: 25) acknowledges that pragmatic creativity refers to "innovation in the context of certain constraints". In his opinion, it is these key words that we should pay special attention to: "innovation" "context" and "constraints". In fact, those key words are interrelated. For Gumperz, "innovation" is related to the violation of conventions, which can also be understood as "constraints" in a linguistic, social and cultural way. Pragmatic creativity here emphasizes "violation" or "flouting" in Grice's notion. Doing or saying something that violates one rule can be explained through another, and as he maintained, "creativity bends boundaries without violating our sense of order" (Prevignano et al., 2003: 25). The key here is "background" and "specific circumstance", or context in communication. In his opinion, it depends on one's "background and specific circumstances" for "conversationalists and analysts facing some input, some cues and so on" (Prevignano et al., 2003: 26) to decide whether they are creative or not. In this case, saying something that is unconventional at the sentence level may be explainable at the utterance level as long as the speaker makes good use of the language and the context, and thus novel forms of utterances will be explainable at the discourse level. Therefore, context plays a vital role in pragmatic creativity.

Paradis (2009: 64) also supports the opinion that pragmatic creativity is not linguistic creativity, but "the contextual counterpart to Chomsky's notion of linguistic creativity within context-independent grammar". In his words, "linguistic creativity" is "the ability to understand the literal meaning of a sentence never heard before" (Paradis, 2009: 64), while as a counterpart, pragmatic creativity in Paradis' view is to understand utterance in context as mentioned by Gumperz, in which literal meaning lies not in the first place but the second. He holds that pragmatics does not change grammar but choose from availabilities, and pragmatic creativity is just one of the availabilities that meet the need of the context.

Based on the above discussion, pragmatic creativity can be differentiated from linguistic creativity to some extent. First of all, linguistic creativity is a term in a systematic sense, while pragmatic creativity is the one in a situational sense. It means that study of linguistic creativity calls for analysis of language system in detail, which can help make clear how a sentence or a word is formed, how meaning can be expressed in different ways, and how grammar functions in expressing meanings reasonably. Analogously, pragmatic creativity focuses on utterance as well as discourse.

Secondly, realization of linguistic creativity requires social convention, whichmeans most users of a certain language come to an agreement in conveying certain ideas. As for pragmatic creativity, its fulfillment requires only the acceptance by both the speaker and the hearer at presence. A creative word or sentence usually complies with lexical or grammatical rules. Even for sentences involving different figures of speech, grammar is the key point before the analysis procedure. However, for pragmatic creativity, lexical or grammatical correctness is not the primary concern. Once the hearer accepts and understands the specific utterance or discourse, and responds as the speaker's wish, grammatical mistakes do not prevent pragmatic creativity.

Thirdly, linguistic creativity is "within context-independent grammar" (Paradis, 2009: 64) in Chomsky's view, while pragmatic creativity is "innovation in the context of certain constraints" in Gumperz's understanding (Prevignano et al., 2003: 25). Therefore, context works as an essential boundary between linguistic creativity and pragmatic creativity. In linguistic creativity, context does not affect sentence meaning, for the key of linguistic creativity lies in word forming, phrase or sentence combination so as to express the literal meaning, in which creativity works at the syntactic and semantic level. While in pragmatic creativity, the key is how a sentence in context can be understood in a right way, how a speaker expresses the idea he or she intends to without being misunderstood, how a hearer can infer the speaker's meaning, and how mutual communication goes successfully in context and so on.

Based on those aspects, we can distinguish pragmatic creativity from linguistic creativity. The range of study of pragmatic creativity in previous studies is on utterance or discourse level rather than sentence or lexicon level. Introduced by De Beaugrande's *Linguistics and Creativity* (1978), in which he concludes that creativity is the awareness of the speaker to organize cognition and thus enables the hearer to re-enact, therefore awareness, pragmatic creativity is taken as the innovation of language communication at utterance and discourse level between speakers and hearers through which communication is achieved. What we have talked about above is the pragmatic creativity in general, as for the pragmatic creativity in intercultural communication or non-native speakers' communication, not many studies have been done. Thus, we will discuss it in the next chapter.

In this chapter, we have gone over previous studies of

creativity in language from several different angles. In each perspective, what creativity refers to differs. Maybin and Swann (2007:515) view that "the boundaries around creativity in non-literary language" or "the object(s) of research" will be settled under no circumstance and definitely will vary as long as further discussion proceeds. In this point of view, what creativity refers to by each scholar depends on the subject that he or she chooses. Language creativity discussed in this chapter can mainly be divided into three aspects: rhetorical creativity, linguistic creativity and pragmatic creativity.

Conventionally, creativity in language study rarely takes situational or pragmatic factors into consideration. Although some connection with communication has been mentioned, creativity in both literary language and non-literary language is concerned more with the creative aspect of language rather than the use of language, especially in literature. In the first section, we mainly discuss the creativity based on different sources of text, which are literary language and non-literary language. Carter (2007: 597) mentions that creativity is now connected with research domains such as "stylistics, literary and cultural studies, second language acquisitions, spoken discourse, corpus linguistics, new literacies, and social ethnography", and we will not review this in detail. As indicated in previous studies, creativity should not be limited to literature. In this book, we will focus on the text from non-literary language creativity, in which more attention is paid to the communicative process. For studies of creativity in non-literary language, scholars mainly focus on poetic aspects or register and speaking styles by native speakers.

Since Chomsky put forward the term "linguistic creativity", it has been under discussion over the past decades. The main focus of linguistic creativity is how language produce infinite meanings through finite sources of language. Scholars engaged in the study of linguistic creativity are mainly concerned about generative creativity and lexical creativity, or we can say creativity at the syntactic and semantic level in general. Pragmatic factor is sometimes involved in the studies of language creativity. Generally, the functions of creativity in native speakers' communication have been discussed in previous studies of creativity from the pragmatic perspective. While in non-native speakers' communication, language creativity has been reviewed in two ways. On the one hand, strategic ways of communication is adopted to avoid misunderstandings. On the other hand, native-like selection in communication is also viewed as creativity of non-native speakers.

In spite of that, pragmatic creativity is not a brand new concept with few scholars setting foot on before, but the efforts are not adequate to separate it from linguistic creativity. In fact, pragmatic creativity is about how language is used to achieve communicative goals in communication other than how language is composed to make sense. In addition, pragmatic creativity is fulfilled at an utterance or even discourse level, while linguistic creativity, including syntax and semantics, is achieved at the sentence level. Scholars who do research on language creativity seldom make a clear distinction between the two kinds of creativity, because it is not always easy to ignore context when working on meanings of expressions or sentences, just as semantics and pragmatics are always intertwined closely with each other.

As more and more studies notice the role of pragmatic factors in linguistic creativity, they act not only as an element, but also a trigger that brings itself to a new research area. Therefore, it is significant and necessary to distinguish pragmatic creativity from linguistic creativity. Pragmatic creativity and linguistic creativity differ from each other in several aspects, including the range of consensus, the role of context as well as the linguistic level where creativity takes effect. All those set a precondition for us to make it clear that research object of pragmatic creativity highlights the use of language instead of the language in use, since the latter one falls into the scope of linguistic creativity. Pragmatic creativity discussed in this section thus refers to creativity in general.

This chapter has reviewed creativity in language in detail. However, there are still some openings left for further research, and questions such as how we understand pragmatic creativity in non-native speakers' communication, how and why they are being pragmatically creative are still waiting to be answered. Those questions will be addressed in the following chapters. Thus, before we go further, it is necessary for us to define firstly what pragmatic creativity is in this study.

# Chapter Three Socio-cognitive Approach to Non-native Speakers' Pragmatic Creativity

Through a detailed and comprehensive review of previous researches on linguistic creativity, we can see that much remains to be explored in the area of creativity studies in linguistics and pragmatics. Since more attention has been paid to linguistic creativity than pragmatic creativity, non-native speakers' pragmatic creativity is still left unattended. Thus, we will put our emphasis on pragmatic creativity in non-native speakers' communication. Understanding the notion of pragmatic creativity is the prerequisite step for further discussion of non-native speakers' pragmatic creativity. In this chapter, we are going to discuss pragmatic creativity with the guidance of the socio-cognitive approach, the theoretical framework for intercultural pragmatics (Kecskes, 2013a: 42).

Linguistic creativity is often studied in a systematic way, which emphasizes the grammatical correctness of forms, while pragmatic creativity is another thing. It is a situational term way, which stresses situational appropriateness instead of grammatical correctness. This is especially important in analyzing non-native speakers' communication. Due to various reasons, novel forms of utterances may occur in their communication, which does not necessarily lead to communication failure. Viewed through the socio-cognitive approach, pragmatic creativity is a result of the cooperation between individuals and the environment, and it can be understood as a contextualized fact that integrates situated speakers' innovative use of language forms and other interlocutors' mutual cooperation to achieve certain communicative goals at the discourse level. Details concerned with this definition will be discussed in the following sections.

This chapter starts with an introduction to the socio-cognitive approach, followed by a discussion of its application in pragmatics. Then pragmatic creativity will be introduced to demonstrate how this approach can be used to explain non-native speakers' communication. Features of pragmatic creativity will be analyzed at the end of this chapter.

## 3.1 A Description of the Socio-cognitive Approach

Since contemporary researches have been highlighting the prevalence of linguistic creativity, various approaches are followed to identify the continuities between creativity literary language and non-literary language. For example, Pope and Swann (2011: 11) list three approaches put forward by Chomsky (1964b: 7), Kress (2003: 40) and Carter (2004: 6) respectively, according to whom creativity refers to "an essential property of the language system" "process of semiotic work" and "pervasive feature of spoken language". In this book, aiming at discussing pragmatic creativity in non-native speakers' communication with detailed analysis, we will take socio-cognitive approach as the theoretical framework to illustrate how non-native speakers' achieve successful communication. Therefore, more attention will be focused on exploring the socio-cognitive approach and how it guides our discussion to our main focus.

### 3.1.1 Origin and Development of the Social Cognitive Theory

The social cognitive theory can be traced back to Holt and Brown (1931) who propose that all animal actions are made to satisfy their psychological needs. Miller and Dollard (1941) make a revision and put forward the social learning and imitation theory. They argue that when a person is learning a certain behavior, clear observations will help to reinforce. Later, Bandura (1977) expands the theory, and studies how behavior is acquired through social learning theory, in which he looks into the relation between a person's perceived self-efficacy and behavioral change. In 1986, Bandura published *Social Foundations of Thought and Action: a Social Cognitive Theory*, in which he formally raises the term "social cognitive theory", which provides a comprehensive theoretical framework for the study of human behavior.

From the social cognitive view, human functioning or behavior is explained through "a model of triadic reciprocality", which constructs the interplay among behavior, cognitive and other personal factors, and environmental events (Bandura, 1986: 18). As a pioneer in social cognitive theory, Bandura (1986) emphasizes the "triadic reciprocality", from which he builds a model of reciprocal determinism. In this model, all three factors influence and operate interactively as determinants of one and another (Bandura, 1986: 23). He (Bandura, 1989: 2) also presents a model of reciprocal causation through a figure as follow:

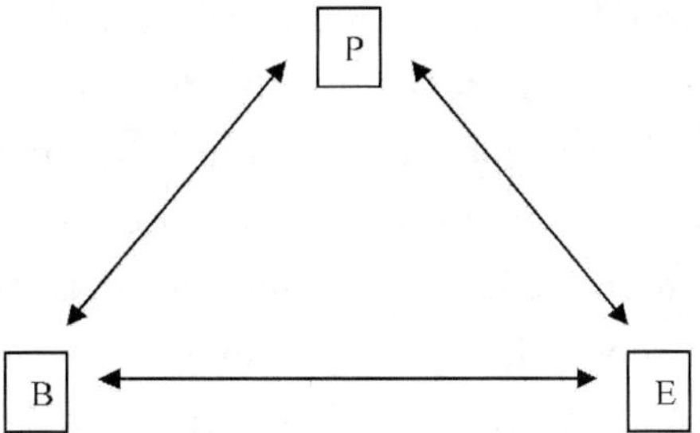


**Figure 1. Model of Reciprocal Causation among behavior (B), cognitive and other personal factors (P) and the external environment (E)**

In this model, the relationship between each pair is reciprocal, and one will influence another bidirectionally. In spite of their interactively mutual influence, neither element is of symmetrical strength in such bidirectional influences, nor does such kind of reciprocally influential relationships occur simultaneously (Bandura, 1986: 24; 1989: 2). Personal factors are defined via some basic capabilities, such as symbolizing capability, forethought capability, vicarious capability, self-regulatory capability and self-reflective capability (Bandura, 1986: 18). Among all those capabilities, the one that lies at the center of this theory is self-regulatory capability, which mediates external influences and provides a basis for purposeful action (Bandura, 1989; 1991b). All personal factors determine one's behavior, and in turn are influenced by behavior. The personal factors can either "strengthen or alter the environment bias" (Synder, 1981; Bandura, 1989). The environment, such as social norms and behavior of people in one's immediate environment (Bandura, 1994), exercises on behavior and provides external origins and supports for self-influences. Bandura (1989) has also pointed out that not all environmental factors will take effect, but only those that have been activated by certain behavior. Behavior itself is under the influence of both personal and environmental factors. Bandura has (1986: 20) stated that "the exercise of self-influence partly determines the course of one's behavior". The influence from the environment offers more choices for people, based on their previous experience. In explaining how moral conduct related to other factors, Bandura (1991a) applies such triadic reciprocal relationship to building a more specific triadic model. In his opinion, moral conduct is the behavior, while personal factors fall into the form of "moral thought and affective self-reaction" (Bandura, 1991a: 45). The two elements together with the environmental factor influence one and another. The application of filling in the triadic reciprocal model of the social cognitive theory has great influence on and prospers greatly in different fields.

As a theory proposed to explain human functioning or behavior, the social cognitive theory has been applied by a lot of scholars to various fields, such as training (Hawley et al., 2010), psychology (Lee et al., 2011), pharmacy (Young et al., 2013) and so on. Different behaviors are detected, and factors that influence those behaviors have been explored. Through applying social cognitive theory, the relation among self-efficacy, outcome expectation, perceived facilitators and impediments in households' consumption of electricity has been explored (Thogersen et al., 2010). What is worth mentioning is that it is not only personal factors, which are of great importance in behavior, are emphasized but also environmental factors are highlighted in the study as a solution. Other scholars, such as Wu and Chen (2013), construct a conceptual model to study the main psychological factors that lead to the cheating behavior in online multiplayer games, and they find that both internal and external factors are influential in cheating behavior. In testing consumers' engaging behavior in online brand community (Kim et al., 2013), such behavior falls into a triadic relationship with consumers' cognitive evaluation of self-efficacy and the positive and negative outcome expectations (influences from social environment). To put it simply, there is a long list of empirical studies that adopt the theory in the related field of research. The above-mentioned examples among the many just give a general idea about the applicability of social cognitive theory.

Not only is social cognitive theory applied to explaining factors that influence behaviors, but also it is treated as a meta-theory for other sub-theories. One of the sub-theories is "social cognitive career theory" put forward by Lent, Brown and Hackett (1994), which provides a theoretical framework to explain career interest and decision-making process. Both individuals (person input) and their social context (background contextual affordance) are important during the process. Through applying that theory, Morris and others (2009) provide strategies for women who intend to leave abusive relationships, and a case study is followed to illustrate its effectiveness. Besides, based on social cognitive career theory, Gonzalez (2012) identifies predicators associated with Latino students' choice of college level. Other studies also aim at testing the model based on social cognitive career theory. Besides social cognitive career theory, other sub-theories are also based on social cognitive theory. When applying the theory to specific fields, the core tenetdoes not change. Therefore, undoubtedly similar cases are not just limited to what we have mentioned above. For example, in social cognitive treatment theory (Riskind et al., 2006), socio-cognitive theory is in accordance with other cognitive theories to treat schizophrenia; while in social cognitive learning theory (Money, 1995; Prati, 2012), social cognitive theory is applied to explain environmental issue like classroom setting and personal factors and so on.

The introduction of social cognitive theory to learning marks "the biggest breakthrough", and its major tenet points out that "learning is basically cognitive" (Eun, 2006: 11). For the academic studies in learning, social cognitive theory explains that the learning process is the interplay of observational learning (self-generated influence) and professional development (external source of influence), which means both aspects need to be emphasized. Scholars who engage in education also support that point of view. Learning is taken as a dynamic process in which context is involved, and an individual is capable of adjusting or, in Bandura's term, altering self-regulatory system accordingly. Therefore, as suggested by Burney (2008), there is a great necessity to offer grade-level curriculum to gifted students. Applying social cognitive theory to learning benefits researches not only in learning but also in accessing student learning. Erlich and Russ-Eft (2011; 2013) develop a model for accessing student-learning outcome through related constructs, and they also propose the hypothesis and verify them. Social cognitive learning theory promotes the development of education to a certain degree by invoking both personal and environmental factors theoretically.

Social cognitive theory has always been and will still be a very important theoretical framework for the study in the field of education and linguistics. When it comes to L2 acquisition, social cognitive theory works more than useful in helping us learn its functions and devices. Based on this theory, Bown and White (2010) emphasize the reciprocal nature of relationships among three elements, which are emotions, individual and social antecedents, as well as how they affect second language learning and achievement. Abandoning the traditional way of research on L2 writing strategies through social cognitive theory, Lee (2011: 48) argues that L2 learning should be regarded as "knowledge acquisition" and "concept development" as well as "a process of becoming a member of certain community". Taking various contexts as the environmental factors and "learner agency" (Lee, 2011: 58) as the personal factors, both have mutual influence on L2 learners' writing assignment. Chandrasegaran (2013: 103) holds that social cognitive model also works in teaching writing skill, which involves the cognitive process of model as well as social-cultural perspective in instructing students to write expository essays.

Applying social cognitive theory to linguistic studies helps not only observe linguistic behavior itself, but also compare Internet conversations with ordinary conversations. Bays (1998) focuses on the social cognitive manifestations of "frame and face", and argues that even though interlocutors are not present when they are communicating with each other, they are still recreating the presence since various conversational strategies are applied based on the cognitive foundation. Koller (2012) analyzes collective identity in discourse based on the concept of socio-cognitive representation from social psychology, in which norms and values, attitudes and expectations are involved. He distinguishes three distinc yet interrelated levels of discourse, and argues that the selection of linguistic features at the micro-level is influenced by socio-economic factors at the macro-level through the discourse (Koller, 2012: 35). Discourse thus becomes the source of data or database for studies in linguistics, or specifically, in pragmatics from the social cognitive perspective. A social cognitive study conducted by Xia (2006) explores the ways of making effective phone conversations especially for non-native speakers. In her findings, she points out the potential of social cognitive theory in pragmatic skills learning, which can be widely promoted in pragmatics. That theory offers convincing explanation to human behaviors, including verbal communication.

### 3.1.2 Socio-cognitive Approach to Intercultural Pragmatics

Social cognitive theory has been widely applied to different fields of academic research, and pragmatics comes as a new join. Although much has been achieved by applying the model, such as social cognitive career theory (Lent et al., 1994), much remains to be conducted further when it comes within the field of pragmatics. This theory has also been further developed as a new sub-theory, called intercultural pragmatics by Kecskes (2013a), which has been taken as the theoretical foundation for the study of intercultural communication.

Socio-cognitive approach has been creatively used as a theoretical base in researching intercultural pragmatics by Kecskes (2013a). It dates back to social cognitive theory proposed by Bandura (1986). In social cognitive theory, human behavior is under mutual influence of the individual and the environment. While in pragmatics, lots of scholars (Rommetveit, 1992; Linell, 1996) have contributed to researching the socio-cognitive approach in exploring conversations or dialogues. Viewed from the socio-cognitive approach, a dialectic relation in communication or dialogical data has been highlighted. Wold's (1992) understanding of language uses functions as the origin of the theoretical framework for intercultural pragmatics. In Wold's (1992: 1 – 2) viewpoint, as a social being, a man is searching for meaning in his own mind within a cultural collectivity, and the process of understanding linguistic meaning is "open and dynamic".

However, the traditional views or dominant tendencies in pragmatic researches are not only from an idealistic approach, but also hearer-centered andcontext-centered approaches (Kecskes,

2010a). For one thing, most current pragmatic theories, from Grice's theory to neo-Gricean theory and to Relevance theory, are all hearer-centered. Kecskes (2008, 2010a) argues that a pragmatic model containing both the speaker and the hearer is an adequate one, while a hearer-centered theory is not persuasive enough in understanding communicative process. In regard to context-centeredness, there are two voices. On the one hand, context is considered as a "selector" of lexical features (Evans, 2006); on the other hand, it is lexical units that create its context (Gee, 1999). Context-centeredness does not necessarily mean that context is overemphasized. However, as an "open and dynamic process", communicative process requires both external and internal context to work together instead of just one. For another, in current theories, too much emphasis has been placed on the positive features of communication, such as "cooperation, rapport, politeness" and so on. It is argued that successful communication in pragmatic view, which originates from Grice's view, is an intention-oriented practice achieved by cooperation, constructed socially and dependent on the context. In this case, personal factors or "negative features" of communication as named by Kecskes (2010a) have been neglected, such as interlocutors' personal prior experience and knowledge, and especially those of the hearer. However, since communication is more a process of "trial-and-error-and-try-again" than "recipient design and intention recognition", taking cooperation as the main driving force and putting intention at the center of communication are not necessarily sufficient to figure out what the communication process is. Both speakers and hearers are egocentric in communication, which means that the behavior of communication is based on "speaker's or hearer's own knowledge instead of mutual knowledge" (Kecskes et al., 2009: 336). Both cooperation and egocentrism need to be highlighted in smooth and successful communication rather than only emphasizing the role of one.

Noticing that current theories on pragmatics fail to describe common ground and even cooperation in communication process, Kecskes (2008; 2010a; 2010b; 2012; 2013a), as well as Zhang (2009), point out that it is necessary to call for a revision of the current idealistic view on communication which only focuses on the "positive features of the process" (2010a: 52). With the guidance of the social cognitive theory, which emphasizes the mutual influence of personal and environmental factors on certain behavior, and combining Wold's proposal that communication is "open and dynamic", socio-cognitive approach is proposed to put emphasis on the relation among communication, context and individuals.

According to Kecskes (2013a), two main claims form the socio-cognitive approach working as a theoretical framework for intercultural pragmatics. For one thing, the roles of speaker and hearer are equally emphasized in the communicative process. Interpretation of utterance helps communication make sense, since it is understood from a holistic point of view. Therefore, the speaker and the hearer are at the same position in language communication, or as Kecskes (2010a: 58) puts it, they should be taken as "complete" individuals probably with varied cognitive statuses. For another, communication is considered to be a dynamic process. Communication is supported and influenced by individual traits and social traits, which are "inseparable, mutually supportive, and interactive" (Kecskes, 2010a: 58; 2013a: 47). He also summarizes some specific traits in each aspect as listed below:

**Table 2. Individual Traits and Social Traits**

| Individual trait | Social trait |
|---|---|
| Prior experience | Actual situational experience |
| Salience | Relevance |
| Egocentrism | Cooperation |
| Attention | Intention |

There are four individualtraits, which are prior experience, salience, egocentrism and attention; while in social aspects, they are actual situational experience, relevance, cooperation and intention. Every trait in each aspect is "the consequence of the other" (Kecskes, 2013a: 47). In individual traits (prior experience → salience → egocentrism → attention), speaker's or hearer's private experience will influence the salience of either lexical or sentence meaning in their mind, which shows their egocentrism. What should be informed is the fact that the word "egocentrism" here does not bear a negative meaning, but shows the speaker's or hearer's salience on "their own knowledge instead of mutual knowledge" (Kecskes et al., 2009: 332). This egocentrism drives attention to utter the meaning or understand what has been said. While in social traits (actual situational experience → relevance → cooperation → intention), intention is, as concluded by Kecskes (2013a: 47), a practice directed by cooperation, governed by relevance and to some degree depended on the actual situational experience. In communication, all traits of the two aspects work together to make sure the communication goes through successfully. During this process, the roles of speaker and hearer change frequently, therefore, an individual is better named as an interlocutor. Understood in this way, the construction of language communication depends on both prior and actual situational experience, salience and relevance, egocentrism and cooperation, attention and intention.

Communication is defined as "the result of the interplay of intention and attention, as this interplay is motivated by the individual's private socio-cultural backgrounds" (Kecskes, 2010a: 58). While for intercultural pragmatics, it is rooted in the approach that combines "the intention based, pragmatic view of cooperation" and "the cognitive view of egocentrism" to understand language communication. We can take a look at the differences between these two views:

**Table 3. Differences between Pragmatic View and Cognitive View**

| | **Pragmatic view** | **Cognitive view** |
|---|---|---|
| **Common ground** | Prior mental state | Emergent property |
| **Communication** | Cooperation<br>(Intention-directed) | Egocentrism<br>(Attention-oriented) |
| **Approach** | Top down | Bottom-up |

The aim of socio-cognitive approach is to eliminate the conflicts between the two views and integrate merits of both views. In the socio-cognitive view adopted by Kecskes, Zhang (2009) and Kecskes (2010a), instead of negating what the perspectives have achieved, communication is better understood as "the result of the interplay of intention and attention, as this interplay is motivated by the individual's private socio-cultural backgrounds" (Kecskes, 2010a: 58). Not only has the role of private and cultural model been emphasized, but also how those models are applied to producing and understanding meanings of utterance in discourse are highlighted.

Keysar and Henly (2002) have pointed out that successful communication requires interlocutors to notice differences between themselves and others; therefore, in Kecskes's (2013a) words, attention needs to be drawn to others' intention, and vise versa. Attention is interlocutors' private knowledge, which is activated or available during the communication process and also helps communication carry on. Such kind of egocentric behavior is influenced by the salience of the information to the interlocutor, and thus it is unconscious. As for intention, Kecskes (2010a; 2013) has emphasized its dynamic and emergent nature. He argues that intention is prior and may "be generated and changed during the communicative process" (Kecskes, 2013a: 50). Therefore, during the communication process, expressing and recognizing interlocutors' intention require attention from both sides. Interlocutors' attention aroused by their egocentrism requires to be recognized in communication, and cooperation is necessary for successful communication. Therefore, in order to analyze or get a complete understanding of the communication process, it is importantto pay attention to both the speaker and the hearer instead of placing too much emphasis on one or the other. It is also not sufficient to focus on the speakers' meaning from the hearers' point of view as in neo-Gricean sense. As highlighted by Kecskes (2013a: 55), this is especially important in intercultural pragmatics since the "knowledge of the interlocutors about each other's background and common ground" is limited.

In intercultural pragmatics, salience is another important aspect worth mentioning if viewed from the socio-cognitive approach. Due to different levels of salience in both individuals and the group, there is a gap among interlocutors from different cultures, not to mention those who speak totally different L1s (first languages). Even in intra-cultural communication, different levels of salience on individual's knowledge would lead to misunderstanding. Kecskes (2013a: 56) stresses that we should pay special attention to the "wide difference in saliency of lexical items in lingua franca and the interpretation of actual situational context" in intercultural communication.

Hence, socio-cognitive approach provides a theoretical framework for understanding the process of intercultural communication. Interlocutors who have similar experience and common ground have a better access to understand each other. This is the same case that interlocutors who share the same first language and cultural background tend to do things in a more similar way. Therefore, it should be kept in mind that interlocutors in intercultural communication share little background knowledge. That is because interlocutors who speak different languages and have varied cultural backgrounds in intercultural communication may bring their own language-specific or culture-specific property to their conversation, which thus may lead to a entirely different understanding of the very same utterance. For example:

(3.1) C: I'm so high today.
A: You what?
C: I'm so happy with you today!
A: OK, when you are happy just say you are happy. Don't use that word.

The above conversation is between a Chinese student and an American student. It shows the different ways of understanding the same utterance in intercultural communication. Both speakers have no difficulty in hearing each other; however, when the Chinese student expresses how she enjoys spending the day with her American friend, the word "high" shocks her friend who is a native speaker of English. Although the American student understands every specific word that the Chinese student is saying, she still tries to confirm what the Chinese student is talking about. The mismatch in understanding what the Chinese student said is triggered by the word "high". Such misunderstanding of the word "high" is due to the different salience of the specific word to the Chinese student and that to the American student. The word "high" is usually used by Chinese EFL learners to express a very high degree of happiness or joy, which is influenced by the culturally endowed meaning to the word "high" among young Chinese people in China; while for the native speakers of English, this word is often used in the context where drug-taking is concerned. Therefore, due to their different prior experience, the salience of the word "high" varies. When uttering and understanding the word, the individual trait of egocentric leads to different attention. Then it is the actual situational experience that connects the word meaning with what the Chinese is saying. The intention of successful communication is thus achieved through their mutual cooperation. Then at the end of this conversation, the American student tells the Chinese student not to use that word if she only wants to tell others that she is very happy.

In a word, the socio-cognitive approach is put forward by Kecskes and Zhang (2009), and Kecskes (2010a; 2010b; 2012; 2013a), who mainly emphasizes the role of culture and individuals in language communication, "explain (s) different meaning outcomes and knowledge transfer". Different factors or traits in the two roles are regarded asindispensable parts in comprehending language outcomes. Besides, the interplay among all those mutually influencing traits also plays an essential role in achieving the communicative intention.

## 3.2 Pragmatic Creativity and Its Types

The relation between language and creativity is quite complicated. The creativity and the research objects vary as scholars shift their subject in discussion (Maybin et al., 2007: 515). Therefore, before we move on to pragmatic creativity in non-native speakers' communication, what pragmatic creativity is in this book should be illustrated at first.

In this section, we will to go over how other scholars define pragmatic creativity and focus on how the socio-cognitive approach assists in understanding pragmatic creativity, and then provide an appropriate definition to this notion. Furthermore, we will try to summarize the features of pragmatic creativity. In the meantime, a general comparison between pragmatic creativity and linguistic creativity will be conducted as well.

### 3.2.1 Understanding Creativity in Language Use

Pragmatic creativity is not a new term in the academic area. For a clearer understanding of pragmatic creativity, we would first see how creativity is understood in language.

The word "creativity" discussed in the previous chapter has been endowed with various meanings. Creativity means "the faculty of being creative, ability or power to create" in *Oxford English Dictionary*, and "the quality of being able to produce original work or ideas in any field" in *Funk & Wagnalls Comprehensive Standard International Dictionary* (1976: 304). In both definitions, the core of creativity is the ability to produce something new and original.

In practical situations, creativity is the generation of new ideas, concepts, beliefs and values that are necessary to deal with our most intractable social problems (Mantysalo, 2005; Stein et al., 2012: 5). Being creative in practice not only means coming up with something new and original, but also endowing an old thing with a new meaning in its specific context. Others define this word as the ability of bisociation (Koestler, 1964) or a personal attribute or ability to be different from the society (Burton, 2010; Prabhakaran, et al., 2014). The main point here shifts from being original to being special and different.

Creativity shows in all aspects of human life. In Rhodes's opinion (1961: 305), creativity is "a noun naming the phenomenon in which a person communicates a new concept (which is the product)". In language creativity, we also acknowledge the phenomenon in which people express new utterance (which is the product). In both verbal and written communication, scholars have different understandings of the term "creativity". Creativity is generally taken as the property of language that users not only reproduce, but also "recreate, refashion, and re-contextualize linguistic and cultural resources" (Swann et al., 2007: 491). In Chomskian (1964b) sense, creativity is a mature speaker's ability to produce and understand infinite expressions that are new to them through finite resources, and this can also be extended to the process of a child in learning his or her mother tongue, as well as the process that L2 or foreign language learners learn a new language.

Kress (2003:40) argues that creativity is the "semiotic work" in everyday "meaning-making" process, in which transformation is often involved. The one-time-use words, such as hapax legomena, rewritten proverbs, sayings and popular expressions in classic works fall into this category. Similarly, Carter (2004) holds that creativity in language is of a wide variety. In his opinion, creativity is acommon feature of spoken language exchange and a significant part in interpersonal communication rather than "the domain of a few creatively gifted individuals" (Carter, 2004: 6). Pope and Swann (2011) even note that creativity may not necessarily be something novel or new, but "a process of transformation" through "re-contextualizing" words or phrases to current context. Creativity is so pervasive in language that it is everywhere, such as in advertisements, slogans, and literary works and so on. For example, merchants always try to attract customers by using all kinds of advertisements or slogan, even a car wash shop, such as the following example:

(3.2) Dirty Car
Dirty Shame

It is quite creative and smart to make use of different denotations of the word "dirty" so as to arouse customers' desire to wash their cars. The word "dirty" used twice in this slogan does not convey the same meaning. The former means something is soiled or likely to soil with dirt or grime, while the latter refers to a kind of unethical or dishonest behavior. Using the word "dirty" is to emphasize the equivalence of a soiled car and its owner's behavior. Such kind of re-contextualization of words or sentences is common in daily life. Besides, innovative words or expressions may be applied to specific context as well, such as creating a brand new word by adding a suffix or prefix. Creativity sometimes is shown in poems, such as the poem written by an international student in an English class to his teacher on Thanksgiving Day:

(3.3) To Linda,
Her Patience to drive me,
And
No matter cloudy or rainy,
Knowledge she persistently giving,
So much warmth she brings to us.

Through applying the initial letters of the poem, the student composes a word "THANKS" to express gratitude to his teacher Linda. Different figures of speech also function as creativity in written language. However, some scholars hold the opinion that the poetic function in language as well as different figures of speech are not restricted to poetry only (Pope et al., 2011: 16).

Other scholars view creativity as a contextualized concept in language, and pragmatic factors count in understanding its meaning in the specific context of use (Lin, 2011; Pope, 2011). Based on the anthropological notion performance (Bauman, 1986; Bauman et al., 1990), Maybin and Swann (2007) develop a contextualized approach to language creativity. In their study, strategic ways adopted by speakers in interpersonal communication have been taken as a kind of creativity as well (Swann et al., 2007; Pennycook, 2007; Cogo, 2010; 2012; Cogo et al., 2012). Previous studies of non-native speakers' communication find that foreign language learners always try to apply different strategies in communication so as to make themselves understood successfully. Creativity in this way thus refers to strategies applied in communication.

Creativity in language is not rare and has been under study from various perspectives, so is its definition. Maybin and Swann (2007) also sort out three ways to analyze language creativity: textual, contextualized and critical dimensions. Textual dimension of analysis mainly focuses on linguistic forms and structures at the word or sentence level. The main concern of contextualized dimension is about how language is creatively used in specific context, and the focus differs in different analyses. The focus in critical dimension is how social relation as the foreground is creatively reflected in conversations. According to the classification of those dimensions, generative and lexical creativity fall into the first category, while linguistic creativity from the pragmatic perspective covers both contextualized and critical dimensions. In summary, besides Chomsky's understanding of structure expansion, creativity in language:

① is innovative forms of words or expressions or structures of sentences;

② and is poetic expression or sentence in context (with different figures of speech).

However, pragmatic creativity seems to go beyond this category. As a comparatively new concept, not enough attention has been paid to it. Through understanding creativity in language, we will explore what pragmatic creativity refers to in the following sections.

### 3.2.2 Understanding Native Speakers' Pragmatic Creativity

Not many scholars have tried to distinguish pragmatic creativity from linguistic creativity. Even for those studies related to pragmatics, the pragmatic element only functions as a factor in utterance instead of being taken as a separated field. In spite of that, pragmatic creativity has already aroused some scholars' attention. Scholars gradually accept that pragmatic creativity should be regarded as an independent research area, and they also provide their own understanding of this term. Based on social cognitive approach, this book takes "pragmatic creativity" as a contextualized fact that integrates situated speakers' innovative use of language forms and other interlocutors' mutual cooperation to achieve certain communicative goals at the discourse level. In the following discussion, we will briefly review how other scholars understand this notion, which underlines how we understand pragmatic creativity in this way.

Gumperz (Prevignano et al., 2003: 25), in an interview, takes pragmatic creativity as "innovation in the context of certain constraints", in which creativity has been limited to constraints. This is contradictory to and in the meantime consistent with the creativity in Chomsky's notion. It is consistent because "creativity . . . presupposes a framework of rule", and "if all constraints are abandoned, there can be no creative acts" in Chomsky's view (1974: 29) (cited by Kecskes, 2003: 136). However, what seems to be paradoxical in Chomsky's view means that context should be emphasized as an independent element, especially in pragmatic creativity. Kecskes (2003: 136) supports that human beings are creative in "rule-changing and rule-breaking", which is the "essence of literacy and discourse creativity". Therefore, creativity that Gumperz refers to is "creative aspects of language use" instead of "the recursive property" assigned to sentences. Generally speaking, creativity is related to something new, something original, but in communication where context plays a role, utterance alone may not be creative, but utterance, or product as indicated by Rhodes (1961), at the discourse level within constraints of immediate social and cultural context can be considered as creativity, otherwise, it would not make sense. The first thing that we get from this definition is that "innovation" in Gumperz's view is equal to the innovative or unconventional forms or expressions, and such kind of forms and expressions should be understood in the context. Creativity here has been emphasized as an individual trait. How to be pragmatically creative depends on the individual, especially the speaker at the moment. In non-literary language, it is not only creativity in language but also pragmatic creativity that plays an important role in producing humor, jokes and so on. Second, such kind of innovation is to achieve certain communicative aims. The following example is a piece of conversation that occurs between a woman (W) and a security staff (S) in a government building. Before the start of the conversation, the woman has just walked past the security inspection equipment but the alarm rings:

(3.4) S: Well, Miss, you have to check whether you have any . . .

W: Maybe it's the belt.

(The woman takes off her belt and passes equipment again, but alarm rings again.)

W: I have no idea.

S: Maybe you wanna try again?

W: OK.

(The woman passes equipment for the third time, but alarm rings again. She starts to check from top to bottom, and finds that she is wearing a silver bracelet. One more time she passes the security inspection equipment, and this time it doesn't ring any more.)

W: Ah, finally!

S: *Wow, congratulations! You won the first prize!*

Generally speaking, the utterance used by the security staff at the end of the conversation is usually applied to situations where someone wins something over. However, in this case, after a strict searching for what causes the alarm beep, the source of metal was taken as a victory by the security staff. The use of formulaic expression that is usually applied in other situations indicates a kind of humor in the above discourse. In addition, it also avoids embarrassment and makes the hearer at ease. The speaker performs a speech designed for a different situation just to achieve a relieving end. This is creative since it gives the hearer a different but novel feeling rather than the feeling of acting stupidly. Through breaking the accustomed use of certain formulaic expressions to specific situations, it makes what Gumerpz called "pragmatic creativity". In daily communication, humor works frequently for different purposes. As in this case, it brings a relaxing atmosphere to the woman, which is based on pragmatic creativity according to Gumperz's understanding. Pragmatic creativity here is constrained by the actual context. What's more, in this case, utterance alone could not be explained as creative, the communicative effect works within the whole conversation.

Paradis (2009: 64) takes pragmatic creativity as the counterpart of Chomskian linguistic creativity, which refers to "the ability to understand the literal meaning of asentence never heard before". In his opinion, pragmatic creativity is to choose from "availabilities" in "language system" under the "given context". The key conclusion that could be drawn from Paradis' understanding of the notion is that the innovative use of language forms or expressions as in utterances need to be understood in the context. For example:

(3.5) A: Dad, I'm Hungry.

B: Hi Hungry, nice to meet you. I'm Dad.

A: Dad, I'm serious.

B: I thought you were hungry?

A: ARE YOU KIDDING ME?

B: No, I'm dad.

(https://www.pinterest.com/pin/558587160004561031/)

The above example is a phone conversation between a father and his child. The original purpose of A is to tell his father that he wants some food. However, speaker B, the father, takes the adjective "hungry" as a proper noun, and so is the case in the rest part of this conversation. The implied meaning of the father's utterance in this conversation is "it is not time for lunch or dinner". B's innovative response to A's statement in a normal context makes the conversation humorous from the on-lookers' perspective. In this example, we can see that a beginner in learning English can understand what each utterance means according to its syntactic structure and vocabulary even if they have never heard of the sentences combined by those words before. The ability to understand each sentence within one's limited language resource is one's linguistic creativity. However, for someone who understands the whole conversation, not only the discourse context should be considered, but also available understanding needs to be chosen from the language system. In this case, pragmatic creativity is built through interaction between the speaker and the hearer. Nuyts (1992: 11) argues that it is necessary for creativity to be in certain order, otherwise, what hasbeen created would be incomprehensible. Meanwhile, each utterance that B produces would mean an entirely different thing, if we don't take it in the context at the discourse level. In addition, it is the speaker's and the hearer's joint efforts that help recognize what the speaker's attention is. The whole process also makes use of sentence structures to achieve their intention. In that process, the role of the hearer is much more emphasized according to Paradis (2009). Therefore, context and pragmatic choices rather than syntactic choices (Kecskes, 2003: 138) are of vital importance.

Nuyts (1992) argues that creativity in Chomsky's recursive property is mainly concerned with how to expand sentence structure in length, which is limited to the sentence level. While for quite a number of linguistic studies, creativity at both sentence and utterance level is involved. However, pragmatic creativity, in which context is highly emphasized, is realized at the discourse level rather than sentence or utterance level. Coulmas (1981: 6) acknowledges that creativity of higher level is "an interplay of grammatical rules, functional adequacy, situational appropriateness, stylistic preference, and norms of use" (Kecskes, 2003: 136). That can be used to explain example (3.5), in which the father takes the structural meaning of sentence instead of its communicated meaning. Kecskes also proposes that creativity here is "of higher level" than that of the sentence level, while pragmatic creativity, though it is not the exact notion he applies, is "using an appropriate utterance in a given situation and connect (ing) it with other utterances (generated or fixed) into a text or conversation" (2003: 138). In Kecskes' (2003) opinion, when making choices from language systems, such constraints mentioned by Gumpertz are meant to be broken by rules. The motivation for making this choice is required as the conversation needs it.

In addition, Csikszentmihalyi (1999: 313) emphasizes that creativity is "a phenomenon that is constructed through an interaction between producers andaudiences". In his point of view, no matter in literary works or non-literary language, achievement of creativity in language requires mutual cooperation between the writer and the reader or the speaker and the hearer. That is what has been emphasized in socio-cognitive approach that the speakers and the hearers who are in equal status in communication should be taken as interlocutors in understanding language communication. He also proposes that creativity is "individuals' product judged by social systems" instead of "product of single individual" (Csikszentmihalyi, 1999: 313). Understanding creativity in this way does not merely depend on the sentence alone, but its context and efforts of all interlocutors who are present. Tannen (2007) also supports that so-called poetic creative language involves not only conversational topic but also interchange between interlocutors. This point of view mainly argues that pragmatic creativity is the result of cooperation or co-constructive effort between both the speaker and the hearer (interlocutors). This is different from what Gumperz argues or the cognitive view that it is the individual's effort that should be emphasized during the process of pragmatic creativity. What has indicated in the socio-cognitive approach is that "communication is the result of the interplay of intention and attention motivated by socio-cultural background that is privatized individually by interlocutors" (Kecskes, 2013a: 47).

According to socio-cognitive approach, the two views (individual effort centered and co-constructed effort centered view) on pragmatic creativity are not contradictory but complementary to each other. The individual effort centered view adopts a bottom-up approach, in which personal efforts have been emphasized in being pragmatically creative in language communication. In this point of view, we can see that pragmatic creativity reflects how an individual is creative in language communication due to the constraints of the context. While the co-constructed efforts centered view adopts a top-down approach, in which cooperation is taken as the main source of pragmatic creativity. Pragmatic creativity is thus co-constructed byinterlocutors in language communication. The individual efforts centered and co-constructed efforts centered view on pragmatic creativity understood in the socio-cognitive approach are named as egocentrism and cooperation respectively (Kecskes, 2013a). Based on such a dialectical perspective, individual and co-constructed efforts are not conflicting in being pragmatically creative in language communication.

Pragmatic creativity is what occur within a contextualized communication, which includes both situational context and individual's prior experience. Moreover, it is the speaker's attention that has been devoted to selecting a specific utterance from all available choices from language system according to the context (actual situational experience) and his or her prior experience so as to express his/her intention. It is the same case for the hearer who is also egocentric, and claims the hearer's attention to the intention, which makes the speaker and the hearer of equal importance in understanding what the utterance in discourse really means. Interlocutors' mutual interaction and cooperation helps communication carry on. We argue that pragmatic creativity is a contextualized factthat integrates situated speakers' innovative use of language forms and other interlocutors' mutual cooperation to achieve certain communicative aims at the discourse level. Look at the following example:

(3.6) Oleg: Well, girls, tomorrow's the day I've been looking forward to for three years.

Max: *You're getting your teeth cleaned*? Sorry, that's what we've been looking forward to.

Oleg: I'm moving in with Sophie.

(*Two Broke Girls*, Season IV, Episode 10)

The above example is a piece of conversation from a comedy drama named *Two Broke Girls*. Oleg is a guy from Russia who works as a chef in a restaurant, while Max is a waitress in the same restaurant. In this comedy, restaurant staffs always make fun of each other with good intention. In this conversation, Oleg wants to share his great news to his colleagues. He falls in love with a woman Sophie from Poland, and living together in whose culture means the relationship will be taken seriously. If someone starts his conversation with something that he has been looking forward to for a long time, the thing must be something important. In this conversation, Max responds Oleg with "teeth cleaning", which conflicts with both Oleg and audience's expectation. Besides, she also explains that it is what she and other colleagues have been waiting for on purpose, which indicates that Oleg has some problems with his teeth. Such conflict produces a certain kind of humor, which appears frequently in this situation comedy.

Based on the above illustration and supporting examples, the following aspects should be taken into consideration when discussing pragmatic creativity:

① prior experience and actual situational experience;

② salience and relevance of the utterance;

③ egocentrism of interlocutors and cooperation among the interlocutors;

④ attention of the interlocutors and intention of the utterance

Taking all those factors into consideration, pragmatic creativity, therefore, refers to creativity in a broad sense, which is to ensure the utterance in context makes sense at the discourse level under the cooperation of egocentric interlocutors. The "pragmatic creativity" that we are arguing about refers toa contextualized fact that integrates situated speakers' innovative use of language forms and other interlocutors' mutual cooperation to achieve certain communicative aims at the discourse level. In communication, the speakers' intention is achieved by means of drawing the hearers' attention to utterance at the discourse level. Pragmatic creativity is realized when illocutionary point of utterance is recognized or identified by the hearer.

### 3.2.3 Understanding Non-native Speakers' Pragmatic Creativity

With the guidance of socio-cognitive approach, pragmatic creativity has beendefined as a contextualized fact that situated egocentric interlocutors use novel expressions or forms to achieve communicative aims based on mutual cooperation at the discourse level. It works at the discourse level, which is supported by Kecskes (2003; 2013a; 2013b) who argues that creativity in language use is not a phenomenon at the sentence level. He also holds the opinion that it is much more than just combining "words or meaning-units" but interplay of "grammatical rules, lexical choices, functional adequacy, situational appropriateness, stylistic preference, and norms of use" (Kecskes, 2013a: 107). Comparing to Coulmas's (1981: 6) understanding of creativity, Kecskes adds "lexical choices" to how creativity should be understood in intercultural pragmatics. From his point of view, speakers in intercultural communication are creative or native-like (which equals to being creative for non-native speakers) if they could achieve their communicative intention and goals through combining "prefabricated units with novel items" (Kecskes, 2013a: 107), which is also supported by Van Lancker and Rallon (2004). Therefore, non-native speakers' pragmatic creativity in this study thus refers to a contextualized fact that integrates situated non-native speakers' novel inputs and other interlocutors' cooperative understanding, which aims to achieve successful communication. It is creative because the novel input actually initiates a cooperative process of joint efforts attended to higher-level goals of interaction. Its novelty lies in the forms of components of utterances that non-native speakers produce are usually unconventional or uncommonly used in daily communication in similar contexts. The novel inputs accepted by other interlocutors could help achieve successful communication. The whole process is based on the interlocutors' mutual cooperation at the discourse level.

Different from pragmatic creativity in general, non-native speakers display pragmatic creativity unintentionally with the deliberate aim. It is unintentional because the non-native speakers make efforts in producing what is required by the conversation, and their intention is not to use novel forms on purpose. The reason why it is a deliberate behavior is that non-native speakers do not necessarily have the whole set or unit of formulaic expression in mind for sure so that they try to recollect what are already in their mind to achieve their communicative goal, which is successful communication or successful information transmission.

For non-native speakers, who share not much common ground, they may adopt different methods in language communication, including either verbal or nonverbal one to make what they uttered make sense or to be understood. Therefore, under the guidance of socio-cognitive approach, pragmatic creativity in non-native speakers' communication is related to how egocentric non-native speakers, who are different from one and another in many aspects, such as cultural background, language proficiency etc., make their efforts to make utterance in context meaningful in discourse. Although non-native speakers share little background information with each other, the realization of this fact requires them to construct the common ground so that they could carry on with their conversation. Even if native speakers are present, the awareness of this situation is the premise for the conversation to get started. Or we can say, what is common sense in the target language for native speakers will even seem to be strange to non-native speakers due to their limited linguistic and cultural resources. For instance:

(3.7) Sophie: Hey, every body! *It's raining cats and goats out there.*
Caroline: Didn't you mean "cats and dogs"?
Sophie: Oh, it's so nice to be corrected as you walk in the door.

(*Two Broke Girls*, Season IV, Episode 10)

The two speakers in the above example are close neighbors. Caroline, who is a local native speaker, works as a waitress in a restaurant. Sophie, a woman who comes from Poland, drops by to visit her boyfriend who also works in the same restaurant. In their conversation, Sophie mistakenly substitutes goats for dogs while using the idiom "it's raining cats and dogs", which means "it's raining heavily". As a native speaker, coming across such an unconventional way of expressing the familiar saying, Caroline connects what Sophie said with the salient idiom structure in

English quickly based on her prior experience and the actual situation that Sophie is coming in with an umbrella. Since she has got what Sophie intends to say, Caroline naturally notices the problem and tries to correct her. Even though Sophie makes a mistake in using the idiom, she doesn't seem to care about that mistake. Sophie's utterance in this conversation is a form of pragmatic creativity in our understanding. In this case, she tries to apply the original idiom but ends up in an unconventional form. In spite of that, it doesn't prevent her from making her communicative intention clear. Even though she confuses the kind of animal that should be used in this idiom, which may be related to etymology, her audience still gets what she is trying to say. Therefore, in that context, interlocutors' prior experience and the actual situational experience interact actively through their mutual cooperation, which makes it a piece of successful conversation.

In both non-native speakers' communication and native speakers' communication, pragmatic creativity is supposed to be the same thing. Still two points make the differentiation between the two. On the one hand, whether it is an intentional or unintentional behavior. On the other hand, the salient difference between them also lies in their deeper intention. For native speakers, pragmatic creativity is a process of interlocutors' interaction in context, during which communicative aims are achieved through utterance at the discourse level. Example (3.3) (3.5) together with (3.6) show how pragmatic creativity works to help native speakers realize their communication. In all these examples, we could see that it is interlocutors' mutual cooperation that helps communication get through and reach a certain communicative agreement. While in non-native speakers' communication, as in example (3.7), the main intention of being pragmatically creative is to get communication through. For non-native speakers, pragmatic creativity does not refer to innovative utterance, as put by Kecskes (2013a: 13), they are creative at the discourse level instead of utterance level. Non-native speakers' limited linguistic knowledge may lead to not "very well-formulated utterances", and moreover, "a sequential utterance-by-utterance analysis (discourse as a process) may not result in the right interpretation" (Kecskes, 2013a: 13).

In linguistic creativity, grammatical correctness is required at the sentence level. As for pragmatic creativity, it is no only motivated by grammar or syntax, but also the social-cultural aspect of creativity (Kecskes, 2003: 138), even if routinized expressions are applied. Creativity in this sense means to apply an appropriate expression based on situational context. In non-native speakers' communication, expressions, sentences, especially formulaic expressions are highly required to guarantee its success. Formulaic or prefabricated expressions have "psychological saliency for speakers of a particular language community" (Kecskes, 2013a: 109). While for non-native speakers, especially when they are limited in linguistic resources in communication, "pragmatics is almost equal to semantics" (Kecskes, 2013a: 121), therefore, formulaic expressions are quite a challenge for both the hearers and the speakers. Once a non-native speaker chooses to use a formulaic expression instead of putting it in a straightforward way, which shows his intention to being native-like, it is one of the ways that is viewed as pragmatic creativity by some scholars. The following example shows how a non-native speaker from Germany display his creativity in use of language:

(3.8) L: Now, the one thing I want in this class is people to be OK with everything, so you never have to say anything if you don't want to, you never have to say anything, so, um, we will start with G, because I know his news.

G: Yes, I was for several weeks, 3 weeks or 4 weeks, I was not here.

L: Oh, you are not here.

G: So because I was not in very good mood, *my battery was low*.

Others: (laughter)

G: *My battery was low*.

This conversation is from the record of an English learning group. A native English speaker L communicates and helps residents whose mother tongue is not English. In this example, speaker G is a man from Germany. As shown in the example, speaker L is encouraging G to share his news with others, and G explains why he hasn't turned up in this class for such a long period. When speaker G talks about the reason, he first says in a literal way that he is "not in a very good mood". Later, he adds one more expression to illustrate his statement that "my battery was low". The expression literally means the state of a mobile phone or some other electronic devices, while it can also figuratively refer to mental state. Such a formulaic expression here means G was not in the mood of doing anything during the past several weeks. Other non-native speakers in the room understand him with no difficulty. What's more, G enhances what he tries to communicate by repeating the expression twice. It is a kind of creativity in non-native speakers' communication, but not what we mean by pragmatic creativity.

The main purpose of pragmatic creativity for non-native speakers is to get communication through. Pragmatics is, as mentioned above, close to semantics for non-native speakers with low proficiency. Therefore, in non-native speakers' communication, discourse often operates in a creative way according to the situational context. Let's take a look at the example below, which takes place at the reception desk at an international conference:

(3.9) S2: And er well i now study my p h d and yah.

S1: All right.

S2: And er well i i came here f- f- for the conference just because i i could er er what would you say er put a a paper here.

S1: Mhm.

S2: Yeah.

S1: You present.

S3: Y- y- you you've got a y- you've h- he's published a paper at this conference here.

S1: Ah.

S1: Oh.

S1: Especially for this conference.

S3: Yah.

S1: You want to present it also.

S2: Well.

S2: Yah.

S3: More or less of course . . .

S2: Yah yah yah sure sure.

S1: Mhm.

S2: More or less.

S3: Yah.

(VOICE, PRcon29: 70 – 89)

In this conversation, S2 (a man from Spain) is telling S1 (a woman from Germany) the reason why he came to the conference, while S2 comes across the problem that he can't find the exact expression to describe what he is doing here ("put a paper here"), he turns to the other speakers for help (" what would you say . . ."). S1 gets what S2 is saying. After a second thought, he offers the word "present", meanwhile, S3 (a man from Germany) also uses the expression that he believes to be the appropriate one ("publish a paper"). S1 obviously seems to be confused with the situation that a paper won't be published in a conference based on her prior experience but S2 is going to publish a paper in a conference based on the actualsituational experience. Therefore, she confirms with them again ("especially for this conference"). After getting a positive answer, S1 makes a compromise statement that this paper is for presentation as well ("also") instead of rejecting the word "publish" directly. After several turns of confirmation, all three speakers reach an agreement that this paper will be presented in the conference. S3 also makes an effort to downplay the need for a conventional expression by a neutral response ("more or less"). Although no newly created words or expressions indicate linguistic creativity in this conversation, it is still creative in endowing a new meaning to the term "to put a paper in conference". It is not only by offering the correct word, but also through negotiating with others to find out what works exactly in that situation. Pragmatic creativity here involves verbal behavior that makes communication continue successfully. Csikszentmihalyi (1999: 313) puts forward that "creativity is a phenomenon that is constructed through an interaction between producers and audience", in this way, what counts as pragmatic creativity is not "the product of single individual", but that of negotiation and cooperation of interlocutors.

Creativity is a puzzle, a paradox, and even a mystery (Boden, 1994; Carter, 2004), and to define creativity is indeed a difficult task. There is not an ultimate definition for creativity that works once and for all, not to mention a unanimous one for pragmatic creativity. It is even tougher to offer an ultimate definition for pragmatic creativity in non-native speakers' communication. In the following chapters, we will discuss how and why non-native speakers are creative in details. Before having further discussion on that, we will look into some other issues first.

## 3.3 Features of Pragmatic Creativity

Pragmatic creativity is different from linguistic creativity in several aspects. First and foremost, pragmatic creativity is a linguistic study in the situationalsense, while linguistic creativity is in the systematic sense. Secondly, the fulfillment of pragmatic creativity requires both the speaker's and the hearer's recognition, while the realization of linguistic creativity rely more on social convention. Last but not least, in pragmatic creativity and linguistic creativity, context is not of equal importance. The most salient difference is that systematic correctness lies at the center of linguistic creativity, while situational appropriateness is the main focus of pragmatic creativity. For native speakers, systematic correctness is usually not separated from situational appropriateness in language communication. However, it is not the same case in non-native speakers' communication. Pragmatic creativity also shares some distinctive features that make it work in communication:

(1) situated relevance;

(2) flexibility, subjectivity and individuality;

(3) effect-orientation.

Let's first take a look at the following example:

(3.10) (A walked up, looked at B's espresso)

A: Is that Peet's Coffee?

B: Not anymore. *Now it's mine*.

(http://cleverthingstosay.com/tag/witty-replies/)

(3.11) S: But the problem is if they eat too much, for old people, you know, delicious food, some kind of.

All: . . .

S: *They deny*.

L: Yes.

S: No, thank you.

L: Yes, yes yes.

S: Could be?

L: Yes, yes, yes, I think also we understand now . . .

Example (3.10) is a piece of conversation between two native speakers. In this dialogue, A is asking B whether the coffee is from the shop named "Peet's Coffee". Instead of answering A's question, B replies that it's his coffee, which creates the humorous effect. Similar to example (3.5), in this case, B also makes use of the sentence structure in the context to respond to A's question. The shop name "Peet's" is correspondent with the possessive pronoun "mine". This piece of dialogue definitely shows linguistic creativity based on Chomsky's understanding, and it also guarantees the smoothness of the conversation as well as the successful achievement of communicative intention. The humorous effect of B's answer in this case is situation related, flexible, subjective and individual. This means that the same sentence or utterance may not be pragmatically creative in other discourses and may achieve other effects. Besides, B's answer is oriented to create the humorous effect. Even in the same situation, different speakers may not respond with the same utterance. In this sense, pragmatic creativity in native speakers' communication is always followed by linguistic creativity. Example (3.11) is a conversation between a non-native speaker S from Burma and a native English speaker L. Before this pair of conversation, they are talking about Asian old people's manner in accepting food offered by others. S intends to explain that old people are modest in accepting others' offering. All the utterances that S applies seem to be unorganized and broken sentences, which do not display his linguistic creativity. However, his utterances do make sense to the interlocutors involved in this conversation. In this case, his partner totally understands what he tries to explain. We could say that linguistic creativity and pragmatic creativity would sometimes be separated in non-native speakers' communication due to their limited linguistic and cultural resources.

### 3.3.1 Situated Relevance

Pragmatic creativity is creativity in the situational sense instead of the systematic one. Discourses with pragmatic creativity in communication are relevant to the situational context, or situation-required. That is to say, pragmatic creativity is not the issue at the sentence level that does not take context into consideration. It is also not at the utterance level, because pragmatic creativity shows the individuals' egocentrism and requires interlocutors' cooperation and "a sequential utterance-by-utterance analysis (discourse as a process) may not result in the right interpretation, as utterances can be attached to utterances other than the directly preceding ones" (Kecskes, 2013a: 13). Therefore, it is at the discourse level that pragmatic creativity calls for situational context as well as both individual and interlocutors' attention and intention.

As one of the main features of pragmatic creativity, situated relevance is not necessarily involved in creativity at the level of text (Swann et al., 2011), such as figures of speech or word play and so on, but that at the level of discourse based on specific context. Creativity in using language, such as pragmatic creativity, is not a phenomenon at the sentence level (Kecskes, 2013a: 107) but discourse level. At the sentence level, lexical choices and syntactic rules are required, while at the discourse level, neither lexical nor syntactic rules are the primary concern. Besides, creativity at the sentence level does not require context as much as or as necessary as that at utterance or discourse level.

Reasons for pragmatic creativity to lie at the discourse level rather than at the utterance level are as below. For creativity lies at the utterance level, situational context is required for situational appropriateness; however, systematic correctness is also indispensable for appropriate understanding. While for creativity that lies at the discourse level, systematic correctness is not the necessity for the appropriate understanding. Another reason is that creativity at the discourse level requires mutual cooperation of the interlocutors involved.

Creativity in language use is taken as a creative process (Bouveresse, 1974), andit distinguishes from formulaic structures through taking functional factors into consideration (Kecskes, 2003). Thus in this case, situation relevance in pragmatic creativity is of top priority.

### 3.3.2 Flexibility, Subjectivity and Individuality

Not only situated-relevance counts, but also the characteristic of the speaker, personal traits, being flexible, subjective and individual. When we discuss the features of pragmatic creativity, it is inevitable that linguistic creativity will be involved as well. Creativity at the sentence level is treated as a counterpart to creativity at the discourse level. It is acknowledged that grammatical creativity is required in generating sentences, while at the discourse level, two more aspects are needed: logical one and social-cultural one (Kecskes, 2000; 2003). Pragmatic creativity is situation-related, and thus grammatical rules alone do not help pragmatic creativity. Kecskes (2003) also mentions that grammatical and logical aspects are constrained by objective factors, but not social-cultural aspects. Social-cultural aspects are more "flexible, subjective and individual" (Kecskes, 2003: 138). Lexical and syntactic rules, the inner core of a certain language, have been fixed before speakers say anything. While in language use, rules of communication can be cancelled according to the speakers' intention, such as speed, volume, degree of politeness as well as many other aspects. However, for grammatical rules, it is not the same case.

Pragmatic creativity as a counterpart to linguistic creativity is flexible, since it is to choose from language availabilities. It is subjective rather than objective, because systematic correctness is not what pragmatic creativity pursues for. While for its individuality, it is because pragmatic creativity is a situational term rather than a conventional one.

### 3.3.3 Effect-orientation

The aim of pragmatic creativity for native or fluent speakers is to create certain communicative effects, such as humor, satire and parody. Pragmatic creativity is oriented to create the speaker-anticipated effect or negotiated effect, and to avoid an unwanted effect arising from the situation.

We can take a look at the following table to see the effects of pragmatic creativity in native and non-native speakers' communication:

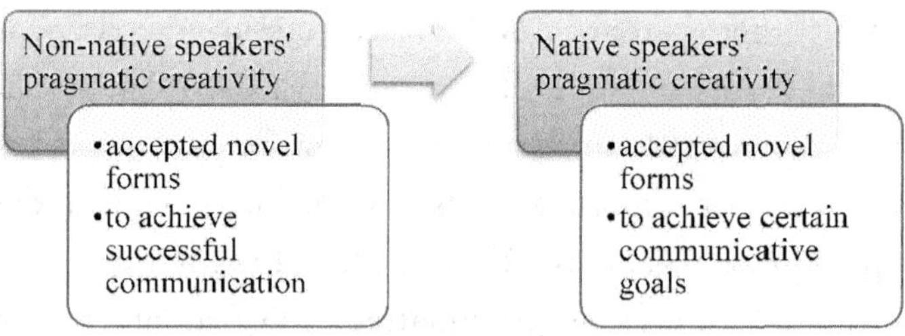


**Chart 1. Different communicative aims of native and non-native speakers' pragmatic creativity in communication**

Pragmatic creativity in both native and non-native speakers is driven by the motivation to achieve certain communicative goals. For non-native speakers, the aim is mainly to achieve successful communication. While for native speakers' pragmatic creativity, communicative goals are of a much wider range. The difference between the two is that the communicative goal in non-native speakers' communication is often at a lower level, for example, to achieve successful communication.

Therefore, as one of the features of pragmatic creativity, the effect-orientation is common for communication between or among native speakers as well as non-native speakers. However, it also indicates that native speakers and non-native speakers areoriented to different effects or aims in communication.

In this chapter, the main focus is on the notion of pragmatic creativity. Several aspects around this notion have been illustrated, including its theoretical origin, definition and features.

In the first section, we mainly review the origin and development of the social cognitive theory, and how the socio-cognitive approach works as a theoretical framework for intercultural pragmatics. No matter in Bandura's social cognitive theory or in Wold's and Kecskes's socio-cognitive approach, an important thing that lies in the core of this theory or approach is that the behavior (communication) is bi-directionally influenced by individual and environmental factors. Kecskes (2013a) argues that intercultural communication is usually taken as a field of misunderstanding analysis. Therefore, when misunderstandings do occur, culture is always the cause. Socio-cognitive approach "reap(s) the benefits of both pragmatic view and cognitive view" (Khatib et al., 2013: 1591), and it is able to understand language communication from a holistic view. In order to know what others intend to mean in communication, both the "communicative function of the utterance" and "communicative agenda of his/her partner" are needed, and that is what the socio-cognitive approach claims (Kecskes, 2013a: 11).

In the second part, we start from the general understanding of creativity to that of pragmatic creativity, and then take a look at pragmatic creativity in non-native speakers' communication via socio-cognitive approach. Despite the fact that not enough attention has been paid to it, pragmatic creativity is surely among one of the most important topics in the area of creativity in language and language use. Pragmatic creativity, different from linguistic creativity in several aspects, can be understood in both a broad and narrow sense. While in this book, we mainly look into pragmatic creativity in a narrow sense, which is in non-native speakers' communication. Pragmatic creativity in this book thus refers to a contextualized factthat integrates situated speakers' innovative use of language forms and other interlocutors' mutual cooperation to achieve certain communicative aims at the discourse level. Pragmatic creativity in general includes textual creativity, violation of cooperative principles and so on; however, it is not the same case in non-native speakers' communication. In non-native speakers' communication, pragmatic creativity is understood as a contextualized fact that integrates situated non-native speakers' novel inputs and other interlocutors' cooperative understanding, which aims to achieve successful communication. This is because non-native speakers are different from each other in many aspects, such as cultural difference, language proficiency, etc. Moreover, pragmatic creativity in native speakers and non-native speakers' communication is oriented to different aims. For the former, different communicative aims are followed, while for the latter, it is successful or fluent communication that lies in the center of its communicative intention.

The situational notion of pragmatic creativity, which is the counterpart to the systematic term of linguistic creativity, shows its own features in communication. As a situational term, pragmatic creativity is situated-relevant in the first place. This means that not only the social-cultural context but also the situational context is involved. What's more, producing and understanding pragmatic creativity requires interlocutors' egocentrism and their mutual cooperation, such kind of situated-relevance presents itself at the discourse level instead of a sentence or utterance level. Second, pragmatic creativity is flexible, subjective and individual. This ensures availability to distinguish from language system to reach situational appropriateness in communication. Last but not least, effect-orientation is not only one of the features that describe pragmatic creativity, but also indicates its communicative purpose. In this process, it is emphasized that the communicative aims of native speakers and non-native speakers when they try to be pragmatically creative in communication are different.

In this chapter, we have discussed some basic factors around this notion, andfurther research should be conducted to get a more comprehensive understanding of pragmatic creativity. It is of great importance and high value to know how pragmatic creativity displays in non-native speakers' communication. In the following chapter, we will explore how different forms of pragmatic creativity help non-native speakers to achieve successful communication through analyzing naturally occurring data.

# Chapter Four Analyzing Non-native Speakers' Pragmatic Creativity

In communication, the speaker's intention is achieved by means of drawing the hearer's attention to the utterance at the discourse level. Pragmatic creativity is realized when an illocutionary point of utterance is recognized or identified by the hearer. When it comes to communication in which non-native speakers are involved, pragmatic creativity refers to a contextualized fact that integrates situated non-native speakers' novel inputs and other interlocutors' cooperative understanding, which aims to achieve successful communication. The non-native speakers do not share as much information as native speakers do with other interlocutors, due to their cultural background, language proficiency and so on. Their efforts, under this circumstance, are consciously made to achieve the aim, and so is their cooperation. The primary function of pragmatic creativity in non-native speakers' communication, especially for those with low language proficiency, is to get communication to carry on smoothly.

In order to achieve this aim, speakers adopt different forms of pragmatic creativity in communication. In this chapter, we mainly focus on how non-native speakers achieve pragmatic creativity in communication at the discourse level through case study. As pointed out by Jones (2010: 472), "what may be 'creative' may have more to do with the strategic way language is used, and what may be 'created' may not be an inventive linguistic product, but rather a new way of dealing with a situation or a new set of social relationships". Language strategies suggested by Jones are just one way for non-native speakers to be pragmatically creative; other than that, there are many other ways that have been adopted by non-native speakers. Pragmatic creativity is the means, while successful language communication (what we mean by successful communication here is not limited to understanding each other, but all smooth interactions, which we will discuss later) is the final destination for pragmatic creativity. Therefore, those forms adopted are what we are going to concentrate on in this chapter.

This chapter aims to give a deep and profound analysis on how non-native speakers are pragmatically creative in communication. Cogo and Dewey (2012: 27) argue that the "setting can affect and shape communication in EFL". In this chapter, analytic perspectives and how we understand successful communication will be discussed, and then forms of pragmatic creativity in non-native speakers' communication will be presented in details with sufficient data analysis. Finally, a conclusion will be drawn based on the data analysis.

## 4.1 Analytic Perspective of Pragmatic Creativity

In the analysis of the communication, we mainly focus on how non-native speakers achieve successful communication through pragmatic creativity. In order to have an overview of pragmatic creativity in non-native speakers' communication, their conversations need to be described and analyzed with close attention in details and entirety, since pragmatic creativity is influenced by both individual egocentrism and mutual cooperation. We adopt the socio-cognitive approach to analyze non-native speakers' communication.

### 4.1.1 Data Analysis of Pragmatic Creativity in the Socio-cognitive Approach

The socio-cognitive approach is a "dialectical synthesis of positivism and social constructivism" (Kecskes, 2013a: 44), which we have discussed in the previous chapter in details. For one thing, it emphasizes the role of both the speaker and the hearer in communication. In the socio-cognitive approach proposed by Kecskes (2013a), the roles of the speaker and the hearer are of equal importance in communication. In order to have a whole view of the utterance meaning, communication should be understood from the perspective of both the speaker and the hearer. This is because even the same utterance under "the same core common ground information and actual communicative situation" (Kecskes, 2013a: 47) may lead to different interpretations by the speakers and the hearers. For another, it is the socio-cognitive approach that views communication as a dynamic process, which is influenced by both individual traits (such as prior experience, salience, egocentrism and attention) and social traits (such as actual situational experience, relevance, cooperation and intention). Therefore, to understand the utterance we need to understand the egocentric personal expression as well as the mutual cooperation during the communication.

We have mentioned in intercultural communication that "participants are creative at a discourse level rather than on an utterance level" (Kecskes, 2013a: 13), while the socio-cognitive approach holds that communication is both "the speaker and the hearer" concerned, and it is a dynamic process that involves both individual and social traits. In our analysis, we intend to combine those two perspectives in analyzing language communication which is a dynamic process constructed through interactional communication at a discourse level instead of a sentence or utterance level.

The data will be analyzed in the socio-cognitive approach at the discourse level. According to themodel of the reciprocal relationship of pragmatic creativity, the context and situated non-native interlocutors (listed as below), the analysis of non-native speakers' pragmatic creativity will be carried out in the following steps:

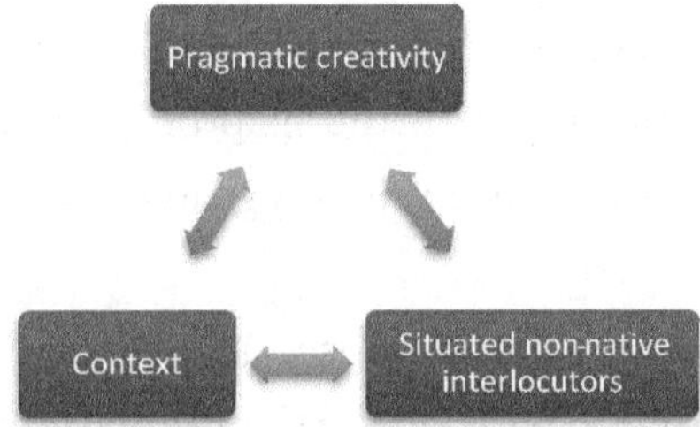


**Figure 2. Model of reciprocal relationship of pragmatic creativity, context and situated non-native interlocutors**

Situated interlocutors are from varied cultural backgrounds with their own "prior experience", and their personal prior experience bilaterally influences their utterance. With the guidance of the socio-cognitive approach, a brief introduction to relevant interlocutors will be first offered. Secondly, it will cover a general understanding of the discourse as well as the interpretation of contextual information, as a holistic understanding of the discourse has been emphasized by the socio-cognitive approach. Moreover, it is the actual situational contexts together with interlocutors' prior experiences that promote pragmatic creativity in non-native speakers communication. Last but not least, forms of pragmatic creativity will be analyzed based on interactions between the context and mutual cooperation of situated non-native interlocutors involved at the discourse level. In this case, unconventional utterances will be under thorough discussion, for the meaning of which is the interplay of "intention and attention motivated by the socio-cultural background that is privatized individually by interlocutors" (Kecskes, 2013a: 47). In the process, unconventional forms or components of utterance will first be connected with a customary use based on the context to achieve successful communication, and then taken as a different or new use to exercise a higher-level function or to reveal any cultural connection as that in native speakers' communication. Understanding pragmatic creativity in non-native speakers' communication is completed with the help of their mutual cooperation at the discourse level in context as suggested by the socio-cognitive approach.

One thing that needs to be made clear before we start to discuss forms of non-native speakers' pragmatic creativity is what successful communication is supposed to be, especially when non-native speakers come to the force. Thus in the following section, we will spare some space to illustrate how we understand non-native speakers' successful communication.

### 4.1.2 Successful Communication and Failed Communication in this Study

The analysis is based on how non-native speakers achieve successful communication when communicating with both native and non-native speakers. However, if we take a close look at previous studies, what successful communication means varies from one to another.

According to Mauranen (2006: 155), successful communication plays an important role in "modeling communication strategies in authentic speech", especially in EFL discourse. Cogo and Dewey (2012) expand successful communication in English in international use to a wider range:

> What we understand to be successful communication does not rely on notions of correctness, assessments of performance or similar factors. Rather, it is based on both a participant's and a researcher's perspective (with particular bias towards the former) on the conversations. In other words, we adopt an ethnographic understanding, and work on successful talk from the participants' point of view. In this sense, successful communication is any exchange that proves to be meaningful for the participants and that has reached the required purpose or purposes.
>
> (Cogo et al., 2012: 36)

In our analysis of non-native speakers' communication, successful communication, as indicated above by Cogo and Dewey, does not rely on grammatical correctness of sentences. This leads us to the analysis of pragmatic creativity in non-native speakers' communication, which is based on situational or pragmatic appropriateness rather than grammatical correctness. In addition, our data analysis will be carried out under the guidance of the socio-cognitive approach. Cogo and Dewey hold the opinion that "successful communication" refers to something meaningful for participants and has "reached the required purpose or purposes". We have no disagreement about how Cogo and Dewey define successful communication. However, what we must bear in mind is that in casual communication, speakers may only have the communicative purpose rather than other purposes.

In this book, we agree with Cogo and Dewey's definition on successful communication, and "the required purpose or purposes" also include the "communicative purpose", in which the speech act of an utterance functions as its situation requires. Thus "the meaningful exchange" is completed with the help of non-native speakers' creativity. The case, in which participants communicate with each other and fail to get the information through, is not necessarily equal to unsuccessful communication as long as it is still on the conversation-going track. We can use the following example to help illustrate this point:

(4.1) M: I want to enjoy myself.

L: Yes.

M: Time, without the baby.

L: Yes.

All: Haha.

M: I just come here, that's why.

L: Ye, one or two days a week, your daughter can watch the baby, and you go shopping, or you do something . . .

M: Haha.

L: You know.

M: *But I couldn't believe my daughter, she is young too, little too, so . . .*

L: Yes.

M: My husband, my daughter, together stay home, I, I, I, I can go out.

L: Yes.

M: But each other stay home, I couldn't believe them.

All: Haha.

The above example is between a Korean mother (M) and an American woman (L). The Korean mother is complaining that she wants to have some free time so that she can enjoy herself, but the problem is that if she leaves home, there is no one that she can completely trust to attend to her little boy. She also expresses that sometimes her elder daughter can help her with the babysitting, but she can not trust her daughter alone if her husband is not at home. In telling L that she can not trust her daughter as a qualified babysitter, M mistakenly says, "I couldn't believe my daughter" instead of "I couldn't be assured in my daughter". Despite the fact that the two sentences denote quite different meanings, in this context, other participants do not misunderstand her, and they are still on the right track of carrying the conversation on.

Since we have made clear what is termed as successful communication in the above paragraphs, it does not necessarily mean that there is no failed communication at all. In the discussions below, cases that are seen as failed communication will also be mentioned so as to better understand the successful ones. There are cases that may not fall into the category of successful communication. The following example is one of the cases:

(4.2) H: In the school, you know, elementary school, that day, Halloween celebration, the student have to wear horrible or something.

L: Yes.

H: Special, special costume.

L: Yes.

V: Maybe your children grew a little bit older, they want you to make costume for them. . . . But not now, maybe.

L: Will you let them, will you let them wear?

M: No, no.

L: No, no? Oh, you, is it, em, is it against the religion?

M: Um?

L: I mean, why would you not let them?

M: (confused, and not saying anything)

V: Why, why not?

M: Why not?

V: Yeah, why not?

M: Er . . .

L: That's ok, that's ok. You don't have to. But I wondered if it was feel like em, not respectful?

M: (no answer) Er . . .

L: I am not sure. I am not understanding. I am not sure.

V：Is that conflict with your religion?

M：Er . . .

V：Is that not allowed?

H：Is that conflict?

V：Is that not allowed?

L：Sometimes, I think some believers do not have Halloween, and some do. Some allow their children to, and some don't, you know?

V：Yeah.

L：It depends. Em, I don't know.

This conversation is between a native speaker (L) and some non-native speakers who are from Korea (H), China (V) and Egypt (M) respectively. They are talking about whether they will let their children wear costumes on Halloween. Seriously speaking, Halloween is a holiday for Christians, while M is from a different culture. Celebrating a holiday such as Christmas in America sometimes does not limit to a certain religious culture. Therefore, L wants to know whether M would allow her children to wear costumes on that day. However, due to the low language proficiency as well as limited knowledge of this piece of cultural information, M does not seem to have understood what L is telling her. Other non-native speakers also try to specify the question in different ways, such as "Is that conflict with your religion?" "Is that not allowed?" and "Is that conflict?" However, M just can't get across what they are trying to ask, and responds only with a perfunctory laughter instead. This conversation ends with no result. Therefore, the topic has to be dropped in the end. In our discussion, this is what we term as "failed communication" as the conversation has to be stopped or the topic under discussion has to be dropped; otherwise, it is successful.

In sum, what should be counted as successful communication in this book is based on whether the required purpose is achieved or not, and whether the function of the utterance is realized as speakers' wish. Otherwise, it is failed communication. In some cases, the communicative intention may not be achieved as it has been arranged, and the topic may be shifted due to misunder standings or low language proficiency. In our discussion of pragmatic creativity in non-native speakers communication, we will mainly focus on successful communication. In such kind of communication, communicative problems may occur, where interlocutors may have difficulties in expressing and understanding each other, but the main issue is that participants always make imperfect lingual-situational matching efforts as the conversation requires so as to keep communication going. In the next section, we will discuss how pragmatic creativity in non-native speakers' communication in details with naturally occurring data recorded from the language learning group and conversations from the corpus of VOICE.

## 4.2 Forms of Pragmatic Creativity in Non-native Speakers' Communication

Pragmatic creativity in non-native speakers' communication in some way is different from those in native speakers', and we have discussed a lot over this in the previous chapter. Due to various reasons, in order to achieve successful communication for non-native speakers, pragmatic creativity is activated to play a role in their communication so as to avoid communicative failure. As Hulmbauer (2010: 343) has pointed out, in EFL, a sentence or an utterance that "suits the users' purpose and helps establish effective communication has the potential for being 'just right'". Moreover, the "traditional correctness criteria", such as grammatical or sentential correctness, does not fall into the consideration of both participants and researchers. This supports what we have discussed above about the differences between linguistic creativity and pragmatic creativity, in which the former appears at the sentence level while the latter is at the discourse level. In addition, for linguistic creativity, grammatical correctness should be guaranteed at the sentence level. As for pragmatic creativity, it is not motivated by those factors but by applying pragmatically appropriate verbal forms to keep the conversations going on the right track.

In intercultural communication, non-native speakers do not have the same frame as native speakers or other non-native speakers from different cultural backgrounds. This would influence their communication to some extent. Due to low language proficiency of the target language, such as the scarcity of vocabulary, the unfamiliarity with grammatical rules or the difficulties in speaking or listening and so on, their communication may be blocked. Taking pragmatic creativity into consideration, what we concentrate on here is not the communication problems but how non-native speakers are pragmatically creative so as to achieve successful communication.

Pragmatic creativity does not necessarily require speakers to be grammatically correct. To violate the grammatical rules is not welcomed in the language system; however, it is also said that violations that may not work within certain rules "can often be explained in terms of another, broader principle" (Prevignano et al., 2003: 26). In this case, successful communication is taken to be the "broader principle", in which way pragmatic creativity guarantees its validity. In Gumperz's opinion, such kind of violation can be captured with "procedures" and "with strategies". The so-called "procedure" is the forms of pragmatic creativity used by non-native speakers.

In the previous chapters, we have stressed that the problems arising in non-native speakers' communication are not the main concern in this book, and what we are going to pay attention to is how non-native speakers apply different forms of pragmatic creativity to achieve successful communication. Therefore, we would like to classify different forms of pragmatic creativity that non-native speakers may adopt in communication based on our data, and then discuss specific forms of pragmatic creativity that non-native speakers adopt with examples in details.

Speaking of methods that non-native speakers may adopt when coming across problems, quite a lot of researches have been conducted in recent decades. Although forms of pragmatic creativity is not the term used by those scholars, what they concern most is related to pragmatic creativity to some degree. This is because their focus is not on pragmatic creativity, but on language errors that occur among non-native speakers, most of which do not block speakers from successful communication. Based on previous studies conducted using VOICE data, Seidlhofer (2004) proposes the following hypotheses to describe the features that used to be taken as errors in language:

- Dropping the third person present tenses
- Confusing the relative pronouns "who" and "which"
- Omitting definite and indefinite articles where they are obligatory in ENL, and inserting them where they do not occur in ENL
- Failing to use correct forms in tag questions (e.g., "isn' t it?" "or no?" instead of "shouldn't they?")
- Inserting redundant prepositions, as in "We have to study about . . .")
- Overusing certain verbs of high semantic generality, such as "do" "have" "make" "put" "take"
- Replacing infinitive-constructions with that-clauses, as in "I

want that"

- Overdoing explicitness (e. g. "black color" rather than just "black")

(Seidlhofer, 2004: 220)

In light of Seidlhofer's (2004) hypotheses, Cogo and Dewey (2012) come to their own conclusion based on the large scale of data from both VOICE and ELFA, which corroborate with the features mentioned above.

- Third person singular zero (e.g. ". . . if one woman have a very ugly appearance . . .")
- Preposition (e.g. "listening music")
- Article (e.g. ". . . there are lot of words . . .")
- Collocation (e.g. "do efforts")
- Relative pronouns (e.g. ". . . I research Bush, which is the father Bush . . .")

(Cogo et al., 2012: 49 - 73)

Cogo and Dewey (2012) draw the conclusion from a sematic perspective, which is mainly concerned with the corresponding linguistic differences between ELF and ENL based on large corpus. The data is picked out through the frequency of a word that appears in the data instead of how a word is used in specific context. Thus, although Cogo and Dewey (2012) have pointed out that the way words are applied in their study can be regarded as innovation, it is innovation in the semantic sense rather than the pragmatic sense. The case is the same for Prodromou (2010: 221 - 222), who summarizes non-canonical idiomaticity in L2 corpus:

- Prepositional phrases (e.g. "on the long run")
- Conversational gambits (e.g. "how do we call . . .")
- Collocations (e.g. "lift an eyebrow")
- Binomials, trinomials (e.g. "dining and wining")
- Colorful idioms (e.g. "a streak of good luck")
- Discourse markers (e.g. "in my part")
- Phrasal verbs (e.g. "hand instead of hand in")

• Colligations (e.g. "take chance")
• Compounds (e.g. "security copies")

Those findings give an invaluable clue for further studies, especially for this book. Although some scholars have already raised some hypotheses, conclusions or summaries, there are still a lot to say about how non-native speakers manage to keep communication going successfully with pragmatic creativity. The following sections will be devoted to analyzing how non-native speakers apply pragmatic creativity to keeping communication going smoothly. With the guidance of socio-cognitive approach, we will mainly focus on the detailed analysis of how pragmatic creativity helps non-native speakers communicate successfully and how they understand pragmatic creativity in their communication.

### 4.2.1 Pragmatic Creativity in Grammatical Forms

In the previous discussion, scholars, who focus on innovation in ELF conversations, are mainly concerned with the hypotheses or summaries on context-independent situations. In those studies, a non-native speaker is only a speaker and there is no exchange of position. While in the socio-cognitive approach, a speaker is also a hearer during communication. In addition, the cooperation between or among interlocutors has also been neglected during the communicative process in previous studies. Thus in this book, under the socio-cognitive approach in discourse analysis, not only is the context taken into account while analyzing non-native speakers' pragmatic creativity in communication, but also non-native speakers' personal position and their interaction with other interlocutors. In the following sections, we will look into how non-native speakers are being pragmatically creative in grammatical forms based on our data. Previous studies (Seidlhofer, 2004; Prodromou, 2010; Cogo et al., 2012) are also invaluable in enlightening this research.

#### 4.2.1.1 Changing Utterance Structures

Interrogative sentences and negative sentences are among the most common sentence structures in languages. For non-native speakers, due to the influence of L1 or low language proficiency in the target language, as we put it, it is always not that easy for them to produce a fully grammatically acceptable interrogative sentence or a negative sentence.

Previous studies have found out that some variations between L1 and L2 in proposing conversational gambits (Prodromou, 2010: 222). For example, L1's version is "how should I know . . ." while L2's version is "how could I know . . ." This is not rare in non-native speakers' communication. As in this case, there is no grammatical mistake; however, the interesting thing is that a native speaker prefers the former form. Besides the conventional way of expressing interrogative sentences, other sentence structures also share the same function in non-native speakers' communication.

(4.3) L: These are from G, and we are celebrating, er, a job he got.
S: Oh, really?
G: Ye.
S: *Where you get it*?
G: Where? In Schenectady.
S: OK, what kind of job?
G: IT department.
S: Very good.

The above example is among L (a woman from America), S (a man from Thailand) and G (a man from Germany). In this conversation, L initiates the topic that G has got a new job. S seems to be curious about how G got his job or the place that G is going to work by posting the question "Where you get it?"

Although there is some confusion in this question, G understands it in the right way. Based on the context, we know that S is not asking for source information of the job but the location where G is going to work. What we intend to point out here is that when initiating a question with "wh-", S goes without an auxiliary verb or copulative verb. In this case, according to Chomsky, an ideal or competent speaker should propose the question as "Where do you get it?" instead of "Where you get it?" as is proposed in this conversation. However, even though what S said is not the commonly accepted way of posting a question, it does not lead to G's failed understanding of what S intends to ask. For non-native speakers, they tend to produce and accept such kind of uncommonly used forms in communication. Viewed from the socio-cognitive approach, communication is the interplay of both attention and intention motivated by social-cultural background individualized by interlocutors. Even though both interlocutors are restricted by their language proficiency, their attention has been successfully connected with the intention through mutual cooperation. For them, an interrogative sentence without auxiliary verb or copulative verb does not influence their understanding of the general meaning. Speakers will accept the unconventional forms in communication, since it does not make much difference in meaning. The uncommonly used utterance applied by situated S and G achieves successful communication. It is the same with the following conversation.

(4.4) S3: yeah (.) er:m (.) we have like er this four presenters (.) hh we have [S2] e:r we have [S8] erm: we have erm: you hh and we have e:r e:r <2> sorry </2> <3> yeah er er </3> [S5] [S5] (.)

S2: <2> [S5] </2>

S5: <3> [S5] </3>

S3：hh e:rm*and* [*S2*] *is going to do the introduction*? (.) < smacks lips > and he is going to say okay the question (.) we had to: discuss and debate about (.)
S1：mhm =
S3：= hh erm: hh and maybe erm because you want us to e:r (.) exactly (.) the words so hh he is going to do that later (.) <soft><un> x<4>xx </4> </un> </soft>
S5：<4> are you going </4> to do the prese- e:r the introduction? (.) [S2]?
S3：yeah =
S4：= yeah
S5：a:h
S2：<soft> hm </soft>
S3：*hh and then he's going to ask*? *erm*: (.) <5> *to the public*? </5> (.)
SX-f：<5><soft><un> xxx </un></soft></5>
S3：hh <6> how many s- </6> (.)
S2：<6> we tried to </6>
S2：we tried to think of it how we're gonna make it more interactive <7> you know </7>

(VOICE：Edcon521：53 - 69)

From S1 to S5, they are from French, Norway, Nether lands, Sweden and Russia respectively, and English is not their first language. Speakers in this conversation are discussing who will give this presentation, and how they can make the presentation more interactive. In this conversation, we notice that S3, who is a Dutch female, poses questions twice, "[S2] is going to do the introduction?" and "he is going to ask? To the public?" In both questions, S3 simply uses the declarativesentence structure to function as a general question. In spite of that, other speakers who are present all show their understandings, and respond with positive answers toward S3's question. In this case, the unconventional sentence structure functions just well as the conventional one in non-native speakers' communication. In the context, S3 puts her question in a narrative sentence form but with an interrogative tone, which is indicated with a question mark in the data. Therefore, from S3's point of view, her attention has been made clear since the tone means a question for her. For other interlocutors present, they also notice the intention of S3's utterance. It is S3 and other interlocutors mutual cooperation that work out the utterance's meaning in the context without interrupting or misunderstanding.

In addition to interrogative sentence, non-native speakers are also very creative in uttering negative sentences in communication.

(4.5) V: How do, how did the doctor say? The doctor say . . .

M: Er . . .

V: It's nothing?

M: Er, haha, ney, no.

L: No medicine?

M: No, er, *no say anything*.

L: Nothing, it's.

M: Nothing, can new, *the doctor no speak*, *er*, *no speak*.

L: Oh.

V: Oh.

H: Is he Egyptian?

M: No, haha.

S: No.

L: The doctor, that's OK, don't get frustrated.

M: Haha.

L: The doctor could not speak.

M: *No finish*.

V: Oh, not finished, oh, may be next time you have to go back again?

M: Ye, er . . .

In the above conversation, V (a female from China) and L (a

female from the US) are asking M (a female from Egypt) about her appointment with the doctor. However, due to M's limited language proficiency in the target language, it seems quite difficult for her to make a complete sentence.What M intends to tell others is that the doctor who takes care of her has not finished the physical examination and has not informed her of any further information. Even though M has great difficulties in organizing a complete sentence, she still manages to get other interlocutors understood. In order to organize what she intends to say within her reach, M uses "no . . ." ("no" means negative) instead of a standardized English negative sentence to convey the meanings. Speaker M is from Egypt, whose official language is Arabic. While in Arabic, to negate the past tense, the negative particle "ma" (ما) is added in front of the verb, and the verb does not change. From the socio-cognitive approach, a speaker utters something based on his or her personal experience. As for M, based on her personal experience, her mother tongue Arabic is of high salience. In addition, as an egocentric speaker, salience always comes first to one's attention. Therefore, M uses the negative sentence structure from her mother language to help her produce what she intends to communicate. On the other hand, the structure of "no . . .", a logic form of negating, is also understandable for other speakers who are present. Therefore, with the cooperation of other interlocutors, M successfully gets the communication through in the context.

Based on previous studies and the above analysis, pragmatic creativity in interrogative sentence is mainly about creating new sentence formats in the targetlanguage (such as using the L2 preferred question structure pointed out by Prodromou), applying uncommonly used sentence structure (such as omitting auxiliary verb or copulative verb) and using structurally unconventional sentence (such as replacing the general question structure with the declarative sentence structure) and so on. While for negative sentence, non-native speakers tend to use the logic formula or insert the native language structure to replace the conventional way of expressing negative meanings. In sum, when it comes to systematic structures, egocentric non-native speakers who are of comparatively lower language proficiency tend to cooperate with other interlocutors, and use the simplest way to convey their meaning in communication creatively based on the situated context.

#### 4.2.1.2 Omitting Lexico-grammatical Features

From the perspective of Seidlhofer (2004), Cogo and Dewey (2012), speakers in ELF tend to use zero singular form "-s". Comparing with many other languages in the world, the third person singular form "-s", the past tense and even perfect tense "-ed" are usually viewed as marked features in English. This has always been a heated topic in the field of second language acquisition. Although educators have paid quite a lot of attention to that in class, it is still inevitable that non-native speakers tend to be confused and leave alone all those marked grammatical forms in spoken communication. It is not a rare case in non-native speakers' communication. We can find similar situations from our data corpus.

(4.6) M: I don't do trick or treat, *but my daughter do it.*

L: Does she?

M: *She go to a friend*, and I not go with her.

L: No, no, she is a teenager.

M: Ye.

L: So she doesn't want mom tagging a lot.

This conversation is between M (a mother from Korea) and L

(a native speaker of English from the US). They are talking about what M and her daughter will do in the coming Halloween. As a non-native speaker, M's language proficiency is lower than that of the native speaker L. Similar to what has been proposed by other scholars, there is a zero singular form "-s" in M's utterance.What M does is that she uses the singular third person (my daughter) as the subject without adding "s" to the verbs ("do" and "go") as the indication of a singular third person, such as "my daughter do it" and "she go to a friend". It is a normal language phenomenon that when speaking in a second or foreign language, non-native speakers tend to use such kind of uncommonly used forms even if they are evaluated as advanced in written exams. This is partly due to the influence of the mother language and speaker's language proficiency. M is from South Korea, while in Korean there is no marked feature in verbs as in English when the pronoun or number changes. As an egocentric interlocutor whose salience is influenced by her native language, speaker M thus creatively mixes the lexico-grammatical feature of her mother language with that of English. Confusion caused by such kind of uncommonly used forms, such as omitting a structural element or grammatical affix, is often accepted and does not affect the intended meaning of the utterance at the discourse level but at the sentence level. Therefore, despite the fact that it is a kind of novel use, interlocutors can still accept it and continue with their communication, which is due to the function of pragmatic creativity.

As indicated in the title, non-native speakers in communication may neglect other grammatically marked forms in English. Some supporting evidence can be found in the following example:

(4.7) H: Last weekend, *I just stay at my apartment and watch the movie in Korean*, and ye at school, this is a parent week, so I am really tied, because it's four days, four days continues, so it's really tied, so last weekend, *I just stay at home*.

L: Where did you go on your trip?

H: Ye, Connecticut.

L: To Connecticut.

H: Yes, but, um, in the weekend day, I have to attend his class, so, listening is very obies.

L: Yes.

H: And I had to conversation, my son's advisors, my son's grading, that's boring, my son school write, so it's very nobious, novols, nobious.

L: Yes, where is he in school?

This conversation is between L (a woman from China) and H (a woman from Korea). At the beginning of this conversation, H tells L what she did the night before the conversation. During the whole conversation, even though the time has been indicated in the conversation such as "last weekend", there isn't past tense in the utterance that speaker H produces at all, such as "I just stay at my apartment and watch the movie in Korean". Grammatical affix, such as singular form "-s", is not the main concern in how to understand the utterance at the discourse level. In understanding the above utterance, if we just look at it at the sentence or utterance level, it is not conventional in the target language. While at the discourse level, based on her interaction with other interlocutors, the speaker L has no difficulty understanding that what H intends to say is in the past instead of at the moment or in general. Despite the fact that H applies simple present tense rather than simple past tense, her partner still responds in corresponding simple past tense "Where did you go on your trip?" This won't make sense without the conversational context and their mutual cooperation as supported by socio-cognitive approach. The other phenomenon in this conversation that arouses our interest is that non-native speakers not only tend to dropgrammatical affixes, but also tend to confuse lexical categories, which will be discussed in the next section.

Besides the marked zero singular form "-s" and zero past tense form "-ed", there are also other forms of pragmatic creativity used in sentences, such as the plural form of nouns in the conversation below.

(4.8) M: Ye, but you are, Chinese is just one, right?

V: Ye.

M: That's why you can do that, but my country is . . .

V: *Has more child*?

M: So you can't be that, and my country is we went to the husband, right, husband family, to go husband family or husband family first.

In this example, M (a woman from Korea) is talking about the difficulty for Koreans to decide whose parents they want to spend the New Year with after they have got married. M is explaining to others the reason why Chinese people would like to spend the New Year with parents from both families. In her opinion, this is because quite a large number of young Chinese are the only child in their families, while in Korea it is not the case. When describing the situation in Korea, M seems to get stuck, and V (a woman from China) adds "has more child?" to help M. The utterance "has more child" is not the conventional way to express what they mean if we see it at the sentence level, not because there is no subject, but the word "child" should be changed to its plural form "children" since it is a countable noun, or the word "more" should change into "a" or "one" if the word "child" is followed. However, if we look at this utterance at the discourse level, we may find what V intends to say is "has more children". Based on the context and what M is saying, M has no difficulty in understanding what V is expressing. In Chinese, there is no marked feature for plural form of nouns. Thus, V's attention is influenced by her salience, which does not prevent interlocutors present from getting communication through. Mutual cooperation among situated interlocutors would help them understand unconventional or ungrammatical utterances in discourse.

There are many marked grammatical features in different languages. When non-native speakers come across those totally different featured forms between the target language and their first or native language, they tend to transfer their native language features to the target language. Although this kind of combined forms in the target language would lead to some confusion at the sentence or utterance level, interlocutors would adjust themselves at the discourse level naturally and can understand what has been conveyed with the help of the specific context and other interlocutors' cooperation.

### 4.2.2 Pragmatic Creativity in Lexical Forms

For non-native speakers, their vocabulary is usually more limited than that of native speakers, and it is even more so in spoken English. Even for those who have grasped quite a large number of vocabularies of the target language, it is often a challenging task for them to use a word correctly or appropriately, not to mention non-native speakers whose vocabulary is limited. Therefore, in communication where non-native speakers are involved, it is common for them to express what they intend to say and understand what others are saying with pragmatic creativity. Non-native speakers tend to use uncommonly used or unconventional forms in communication, such as omitting the third person singular form in English; while for lexicons, merely shifting from the first language to the target language does not seem to work. In the following sub-sections, we are going to discuss how non-native speakers creatively make communication go through by lexical forms of pragmatic creativity.

#### 4.2.2.1 Shifting Lexical Functions

Part of speech is an important classification in almost every language. While in English, we can see that there are specific places in a sentence structure that different kinds of part of speech can fit into. Some parts of speech in English are quite simple for non-native speakers to match with their first languages, such as adjectives, adverbials and so on, while others are not. For example, in ELF communication, definite and indefinite articles are often employed in innovative ways (such as "lot of") (Cogo et al., 2012: 61). Besides the innovative use of articles, there are other creative ways of language use in non-native speakers' communication. Non-native speakers in actual situations often apply various verbs and nouns, the most essential parts of speech in a language, creatively to get communication through.

At the end of the example (4.6), we mentioned another phenomenon, which is also worthy of our attention.

(4.9) H: Last weekend, I just stay at my apartment and watch the movie in Korean, and ye at school, this is a parent week, so I am really tied, because it's four days, four days continues, so it's really tied, so last weekend, I just stay at home.

L: Where did you go on your trip?

H: Ye, Connecticut.

L: To Connecticut.

H: Yes, but, um, in the weekend day, I have to attend his class, so, listening is very obies.

L: Yes.

H: *And I had to conversation*, my son's advisors, my son's grading, that's boring, my son school write, so it's very nobious, novols, nobious.

L: Yes, where is he in school?

Despite the fact that the non-native speaker H has omitted the grammatical affix inher utterance, she also innovates a new use of the part of speech. In the above conversation, H says that "*and I had to conversation*, my son's advisors, my son's grading, that's boring". It is not a complete or conventional sentence, since no predicate but a noun follows the phrase "had to". If we take a deep look at this utterance, it is not difficult to tell that H intends to use the noun "conversation" as a verb or verbal phrase such as "talk" or "have a conversation with". In this case, the noun "conversation", which has been privatized by H, functions as a verb. In such context, there is no difficulty for others to work out H's intention in the conversation.

Except that non-native speakers use nouns as verbs to convey what they intend to, they also treat a verb as a noun.

(4.10) C: He saw their teacher had the nail polished, he said, maybe I can have the polish. I said, no, that's for girls.*But he don't care my disagree*. He said, one of my classmates, he is a boy, he do that too. I said, may be other people, not you.

L: Yes.

C: I think they just feel it's really fun, I think. You know, he said his teacher has well polished long nails, he said it's hard for Ms. X to tie the shoe for the kids.

All: . . .

In this conversation, C (a mother from China) is talking about some interesting things that happened to her elder son, while others are just listening, without making any comment. L (a woman from America) also shows her confirmation on the information by just saying "yes". There are some grammatical forms of pragmatic creativity in C's utterance, such as the omitting of the third person singular form; however, this is not what we are paying attention to in the above conversation. What interests us is the shifting function of a verb into a noun in C's utterance. C is talking about her son who prefers to have his nails polished, which she does not agreewith. Her son, with reasonable excuses, ignore her opposition at first. In C's utterance, she uses "my disagree" instead of "my disagreement" or "my opposition" to express what she intends to. There is not many differences in the noun form and verb form of a word denoting to the same meaning in Chinese as that in English. As a non-native speaker from China, C, who is an egocentric interlocutor as one of the individual traits mentioned in socio-cognitive approach, creatively uses the word stem (the verb form here) to help communication through. In this case, other speakers all accept the shifting of the lexical function. Through their mutual cooperation, C's attention is intertwined with their attention, which helps achieve successful communication.

There is not only shifting between different parts of speech, but also shifting within one part of speech in non-native speakers' communication, such as the innovative use of definite and indefinite articles. Other than that, the two kinds of verbs in English, transitive verb and intransitive verb, fall into the latter category as well. Transitive verb refers to the kind of verb that can be followed by one or more objects, while intransitive verb refers to the kind of verb that does not have any objects unless a preposition follows the verb. A verb in English can be transitive, intransitive or ambitransitive. In spite of that, this does not necessarily cause confusions for non-native speakers in communication, when pragmatic creativity in lexicon functions.

(4.11) L: Did you drive in the snow?
M: No.
L: No, you have to be very careful.
M: Ye.
L: Because you will slide.
M: Ye, ye, *my husband tell*.
L: And when you ski, do you know what I mean, the car ski.

This conversation happens between L (a woman from China) and M (a woman from Egypt). They are talking about driving skills in snowy weather. As a non-native speaker, M's language proficiency is undoubtedly lower than that of the native speaker L. Based on what M says, we can find uncommonly used language forms in M's utterance, such as omitting zero singular form "-s" or past form "-ed", which we have discussed above. However, except for the person or tense in the predicate, another problem arouses our interest. In this case, there is no doubt that "tell" is used as a verb. However, when "tell" is used as an intransitive verb, it is mainly used to refer to three situations. The first one is to say something since there might be a certain sign that indicates it, such as in "He might have been lying. I can't tell". Secondly, it occurs when someone reports bad behaviors that others have done. Thirdly, it is used to describe certain harmful effects on someone. Although M's utterance does not show any mistake or inappropriateness at the sentence level, the problem is that it does not mean what she intends to convey. In spite of that, other interlocutors present have no comment on the way she shifts the part of speech of "tell" from a transitive verb to an intransitive one. Pragmatic creativity in this case is achieved through the internal shift of part of speech. With the guidance of the socio-cognitive approach to the understanding of pragmatic creativity, shifting part of speech in utterance at the discourse level is understandable for situated interlocutors through their mutual cooperation.

In spoken communication, speakers show their pragmatic creativity through many forms. Shifting part of speech is one of them. As one of the pragmatic creativity forms, class shift is not just limited to various parts of speech, such as noun to verb or verb to noun, but also within certain part of speech itself, such as mixed use of transitive and intransitive verb. The shift of part of speech is mainly caused by non-native speakers limited vocabulary or low language proficiency. It is also the reason why non-native speakers are more pragmatically creative in communication for the purpose of getting communication to carry on.

#### 4.2.2.2 Using an Alternative Word

Using an alternative word means to use a word that is not so proper in the exact context as substitution for the appropriate one. The relation between these two words may be synonyms, near-synonyms or even hyponyms of the same superordinate term. Similar to shifting part of speech, using an alternative word is another form of pragmatic creativity for non-native speakers to achieve successful communication. Compared with shifting part of speech, it is more creative and also easier for non-native speakers in communication to express what they intend to by using an alternative word. It is also an important form of pragmatic creativity that non-native speakers who are of low language proficiency will use to get communication through.

In this process, notional words instead of functional words are prone to be substituted by alternative words. For example, words not salient in gender frequently replace words that indicate marked gender in communication. In spoken language, non-native speakers tend to use "he" to refer to gender in general. Thisis common in our data, especially for non-native speakers from China and Korea. For example,

(4.12) F: Haha, my daughter is 10 years old.

L: Really?

F: This is her first day to go to the school.

L: Oh.

F: The elementary school.

L: 10 years old, is she in 4th or 5th grade?

F: Er, 5th grade.

L: OK.

F: *This is the first day he go to the new school.*

L: How was it?

F: *He was exciting, but yesterday night, yerster night, he, er, she couldn't sleep.*

All: Hahaha.

L: Excited.

F: But she after the class, I pick her up, her, at the street, the school bus stop, so *she was very exciting.*

L: Oh.

F: She told us about, lots things about school.

L: Good.

F: The classmate, the teacher and dededede . . . so, so, so, she met . . .

In this conversation, F (a mother from China) is sharing about her daughter's new life in America with L (a native speaker of English from the US) and other non-native speakers who are from different countries. At the beginning of the conversation, F uses the possessive pronoun "her" which indicates her daughter's gender. However, when it comes to the pronoun, F seems to have left the difference of gender in pronoun behind. It is not until the third time when F comes across the pronoun does she realize the exact word that she should use to refer to her daughter is "she" rather than "he". In spite of that, interlocutors in this conversation do not seem to be confused about what F is trying to convey. Another point in this conversation that we should pay attention to is F's utterances "he was exciting" and "she was very exciting". In this conversation, L tries to replace F's expression with the word "excited", which is generally used to describe people's subjective mood. This indicates that the unconventional form that F uses here does not confuse others at all. If we look at this conversation at the sentence level, we can notice that it is a process of making mistakes, correcting and making mistakes again. However, if we switch to the discourse level, we can find that no misunderstanding occurs during the communication. The non-native speaker F has privatized pragmatic creativity in the form of alternative words in communication, and her intention is recognized by other interlocutors present. Non-native speakers' flexible use of possessive nouns and adjectives is achieved with the help of other non-native speakers' cooperation in the very context.

Other cases in our data also show how non-native speakers use an alternative adjective to replace the appropriate or more conventional one so as to achieve successful communication.

(4.13) S6: er from er (.) the <spel> p h d </spel> er to er (.) an (associate) professorship (1) there is er still some (1) kind of er (2) erm restricted er (1) time at the university for (.) three of six years and er you have to finish your second er (1) erm (1) <spel> p h d</spel> you can say (.) <pvc> habilitation </pvc> degree and then

SX-m: <soft> (aha) </soft> (1)

S6: then you can apply for er (.) (associate) professorships or for full professorships <soft><un> xx </un></soft>

S5: <soft> a:h </soft> (.)

S6: typically you you apply for (associate) professorships

(.) and only the (associate) professorships they are er (.) and the full professorships hh they're for a lifetime positions (1)

S5: <soft> a:h </soft>

S6: so all the other are (2) only for some (.) how how do you call that in english? (1)

SX-m: @ (.) @@ (1)

S7: <L1ger> was meinen (sie) = {what do you mean} </L1ger>

S6: <L1ger> = zeitvertraege? {fixed-term contracts} </L1ger> (2)

S7: erm (2)*time-limited*? =

S6: = time-limited?

S5: @@ <5> @@ </5>

S6: <5> @@ </5> @@ okay =

(VOICE: PRcon599: 40 – 53)

In the above conversation, S5 (a male from Korea), S6 (a male from Germany) and S7 (a male from Germany) are talking about positions at universities in different countries. At first, S6 is explaining the procedure for a PhD to become an associate professor and then get a full professorship. He also points out that full professorship is a lifetime position, while others are not. However, when describing something opposite to "lifetime", S6 has difficulties in finding the corresponding word to express the idea. Therefore, he asks others for help. S7, whose L1 is also German, asks S6 what he means in German. After they negotiate with each other in German for a round, S7 offers a word "time-limited". Based on the context in the discourse, the word S7 is looking for is the antonym for "lifetime", which is supposed to be "temporary" or "short-term". However, S7 seems to have difficulty in finding the appropriate word, and thus turns to the alternative word "time-limited" for substitution. Although "time-limited" is not the exact word that S7 looks for in this conversation and also not what S6 totally agrees with based on their negotiation, S5 gets it and S6 also makes compromise to it. In this case, the relationship between the adjective used and the most appropriate one in the context is near-synonyms. Although the word used in the conversation is not the appropriate one in that context, after the interplay of the speaker S7's attention and intention, such kind of lexical form of pragmatic creativity guarantees the successful communication through their mutual cooperation.

Creative use of other notional words, such as nouns and verbs, can also be found in our data.

(4.14) L: Hi, K!
K: Oh, hi! I like your hair.
L: Thank you, where are you heading?
K: To the library.
L: Oh, then you'd better hurry up, it's really cold outside.
K: Ye, where are you going?
L: *I am going to the campus center to have ... er, dinner.*
K: Oh, have a good lunch!

This is a piece of daily conversation between two students. K (a female student from Kazakhstan) and L (a female student from China) are greeting each other around 12 o'clock at noon. L gets stuck when she tries to tell K what she is going to do. Under such circumstance, she quickly comes up with the expression of "have dinner" instead of "have lunch", which is more appropriate in that context. Although the word "dinner" could be used as the meal in the midday, it is inaccurate to be applied here since L is only going to have a meal in the school's dinning room. As a non-native speaker, K accepts L's creative use of the words and understands her words without any difficulty. It is their cooperation in that context that helps the communication go on successfully. The words "dinner" and "lunch" in general differ from each other in two aspects. On the one hand, "dinner" usually refers to the meal in the evening, while "lunch" is the meal people have at noon. On the other hand, "dinner" is comparatively more formal than "lunch", and thus, a formal meal at noon can also be called "dinner". In spite of these differences, both words indicate a meal, no matter when or whether it is formal or informal. It is the similarity of the two words that leads to non-native speakers' creative use in this conversation. Although the two words can be taken as near-synonyms, the meaning of the word "dinner" has been expanded by speaker L, covering the range of "casual lunch" in this case, and speaker K accepts such privatized use of the word. Other situations also involve using alternative nouns in our data. The following case is one of the examples.

(4.15) H: I have to, I am thinking about that, I, so I talk to my friend with my friend beside, one day, *we memorize one chapter one day.*

L: One verse, one little.

H: *One chapter.*

L: A whole chapter?

H: *not the whole chapter, we have . . .*

L: Ye.

H: We have some little bit . . .

L: Oh, OK.

H: Yes.

L: OK, a little bit of the chapter.

H: Yes.

L: Yes.

In this conversation, H (a woman from Korea) is telling others that she is betting with her friends about reciting a part of a chapter of the Bible each day. If any of them do not finish what has been required, they will lose 10 dollars. At the beginning of this conversation, what H says is "one chapter one day" which astonished L (a woman from America). We know that to recite one chapter of the Bible is quite a tough job for ordinary people. That's why L feels it quite confusing and unbelievable, and then she changes what H says into "one verse". However, H negates what L suggests and insists on using the word "one chapter". Therefore, L again questions about whether they could memorize one chapter a day by asking"A whole chapter?" H notices that it should not be the whole chapter, but "some little bit". After confirming with H, L is also satisfied with the result that H memorizes "a little bit of the chapter" instead of "the whole chapter", which is more reasonable. The process of negotiation helps match what is privatized by the non-native speaker with its intended function in communication. In this case, the word meaning of "chapter" has been reduced to "verse". Synonyms are most frequently used as alternative choices. As for near synonyms, the relationship between the general meaning of the most appropriate word in the context and that of the word used is not only partly overlapping, but also with comparatively wide and limited range in reference. This is not just the case for nouns, but also that for verbs.

(4.16) M: I want to enjoy myself.

L: Yes.

M: Time, without the baby.

L: Yes.

All: Haha.

M: I just come here, that's why.

L: Ye, one or two days a week, your daughter can watch the baby, and you go shopping, or you do something.

M: Haha.

L: You know.

M: *But I couldn't believe my daughter*, she is young too, little too, so . . .

L: Yes.

Me: My husband, my daughter, together stay home, I, I, I, I can go out.

L: Yes.

M: But each other stay home, *I couldn't believe them.*

All: Haha.

We have illustrated the above example when defining successful communication. The reason why it is worth mentioning here again is to support the idea that the pragmatic creativity form of using an alternative word in the specific context indeed helps non-native speakers achieve successful communication. When telling L that she can not trust her daughter as a qualified babysitter, M says, "I couldn't believe my daughter" and "I couldn't believe them" instead of "I couldn't be assured in my daughter/them". In the form of using an alternative word, there is no grammatical mistake in non-native speakers' utterance; however, the only problem is that the word used in the exact conversational context is not so appropriate or conventional. Although the word "believe" and "trust" are synonyms to each other, the former only refers to taking what someone says or does as truth, while the latter means to have faith in someone. In this case, the meaning that M intends to convey is embodied in the latter, but she uses the former. Despite the fact that the two sentences denote quite different meanings, the other participants do not misunderstand what M is expressing in such a context, but stay on the conversation-going track.

As for verbs, not only synonyms, but also near-synonyms exist in our data.

(4.17) L: What did you like best?

Y：I like，er，they are ready for turkey and some salmon.

L：Oh.

Y：And stuffing，I like turkey and salmon.

L：Yes，yes，mash potatoes?

Y：Mash potato，yes，but I can't enjoy it，because my son，and . . .

V：Haha.

L：(Knocking the table) He is like this?

Y：He doesn't want to eat，and *I am trying*，*trying to eat her*.

V：Feed her，feed her.

L：Yes.

Y：Feed her，ye，ye. He doesn't want eat.

L：Oh.

Y：So.

L：Oh，haha.

Y：So I am just take a little.

In this piece of data，Y (a mother from Korea) is complaining to V (a woman from China) and L (a woman from America) that her son did not behave well when she and her husband went to her friends' house for the Thanksgiving dinner. Under that circumstance，she had no choice but to feed her son so that she had little food during the feast. What Y intends to express is that she spends most of her time feeding her son. However，in their communication，what she actually says is "I am trying to eat her". This is definitely unacceptable in the immediate context，since the pronoun "her" here denotes to Y's son. This is far away from what she actually means at the utterance level. But at the discourse level，interlocutors are easy to figure out what she really means，even though Y uses "her" instead of "him" as the object of the verb "eat". Therefore，V tries to correct what she says and make their communication less awkward. The two words "eat" and "feed" are similar to each other when referring to the action of taking food. While the difference lies in that "to eat" is an active behavior of taking food in, while "to feed" is the other way around. Thus, the receiver of "eat" is food, while that of "feed" is someone. In the example, based on the context, Y connects the similarity between those two words while overlooking the difference, in which way she creatively leads other interlocutors to understand what she is trying to convey. In the point of view of socio-cognitive approach, such smooth communication with inappropriate words is achieved based on situated interlocutors' cooperation at the discourse level.

Besides adjective synonyms and near-synonyms, non-native speakers also apply unconventional words or expressions that are even beyond near-synonyms to get communication through.

(4.18) L: Were you surprised to see snow this morning?
M: Mm . . .
L: I was, it's cold, it's cold, like . . .
S: Really, really.
G: *Delicious, delicious, I am fine, I am fine.*
L: Are you trying?
H: Delicious?
All: Hahaha.
H: You didn't, you first time you see the . . .
G: Ye, ye.
H: The snow.
G: Ye.
S: He like it, he like the snow, there you will see, hum . . .
All: Haha.
L: Ye, right, right, oh, well.

The conversation takes place among several non-native speakers and a native speaker (L). They are talking about the snowy weather the day before. Everyone is surprised at the snow.

M (a woman from Korea) confirms with "mm", and S (a man fromBurma) agrees with "really, really", while G (a man from Thailand) surprisingly replies with "delicious, delicious, I am fine, I am fine". G's reply is almost nonsense even if we don't separate the question from its answer. The answer "delicious, delicious, I am fine, I am fine" does not match the question "Were you surprised to see snow this morning?" at all. However, if we take a further look at their following conversation, H (a woman from Korea) shows her confusion at the first moment when she hears the answer, and she then immediately connects the actual situation that G is from Thailand. According to her prior experience, Thailand is a country without any snow all the year around, and this is the first snow of the year in this place. The second step she does is to confirm her supposition. There is no correcting or revising in this case, since both the prior experience and the actual situational context help others to accept the unconventional expression used here. In addition, although what G says doesn't make sense, which is caused by his low language proficiency, all the words he uses deliver a positive meaning. All of those positive words or expressions transmit the message that he is well with the snow. Viewed from the socio-cognitive approach, those alternative words used do not prevent non-native speakers from understanding each other. In this case, the appropriate word and the word invited by the non-native speaker are close to hyponyms of the same superordinate term, both of which are used to describe positive aspects.

Cases of word meanings that are not so close can also be found in using alternative nouns and verbs, which are beyond near synonyms, but hyponyms of the superordinate term.

(4.19) L: So where do you get protein? Tofu?

I: Tofu?

(All of the rest shake their head.)

L: You don't know tofu?

V: Oh, I know, it's bean curd.

I: No. (still shake her head)

V: *How about soybean*?

I: Oh, soybean, ye ye.

The above conversation happens among L (a woman from America), I (a woman from India), V (a woman from China) and some other interlocutors. They are talking about vegetarians. L is asking I, who happens to be a vegetarian, how they get protein from their diet. When asked "(do you get protein from) tofu?" I, obviously confused by this word, does not give an anticipated answer. Receiving no answers from her, L wants to make sure if her confusion is due to the strangeness with the word or not. Under that circumstance, V tries to provide a synonym of tofu (bean curd) to help with the situation, but still ends in failure. Then, she changes the concept a little bit and gives it a third try with the word "soybean" which is the raw material for making tofu and bean curd. With this word, I is able to figure out what she is referring to, and their conversation goes on further. In this conversation, in order to help the non-native speaker I build some connection between the concept of protein and tofu, V first applies a synonym, and then turns to its material, which can be understood as a hyponym to "tofu". Although non-native speakers' communication is limited by their language proficiency, they are capable of achieving successful communication through active mutual cooperation and creatively contextualizing word's meaning. This is especially obvious in notional words.

Non-native speakers also apply substitution verbs beyond near synonyms to help them get communication through.

(4.20) S2: <soft> i'm looking </soft> (3) okay (1) <to S7 > [S7] what's <LNger> ausweichen? {to swerve}

</LNger> </to S7 > (.) < soft > okay she's reading </soft>(.) <to S3> what's <LNger> ausweichen? {to swerve} </LNger ></to S3 > (1)

S3: <soft> erm (2) er er @@ (it's like) </soft>

S2: <loud> it's like the example is? (.) er <LNger> der radfahrer ist dem auto ausgewichen. {the cyclist gave way to the car} </LNger></loud> (.)

S3: yeah i (.) i know what you mean (1) <un> xx </un>

S2: *it's like to change?*

S3: hm?

S1: no:

S9: <5>*somehow* </5> *to change*

S3: <5> no it's like </5>

S3: *if you if you SWERVE* (.) you wanna you wanna go past something and then (1)

S1: *SUEEZE* ?

S3: you change yea:h (.) you <6> you change </6> PATH .

S1: <6> change the </6>

S1: okay the <7> the </7> okay

S2: <7> okay </7>

S3: <7> yeah </7>

S3: (but) that's probably not the correct <1> word </1>

S1: *<loud><1> to </1> OMIT* ? (1) *to omit? </loud> right?* =

S3: = yeah

S1: okay

S3: yeah (3)

(VOICE: EDcon4: 763 – 783)

In this piece of conversation, S2 (a woman from Romania), whose first language is Romanian, comes across the difficulty of expressing the meaning of "swerve" in English. However, since this conversation takes place in Vienna, where the officiallanguage is German instead of English, no interlocutor present shares the same L1 with S2. Thus, S2 chooses to use the local official language, because it is much easier to find the corresponding word in German for her. During the process of negotiation, S2 figures out several words to convey the meaning of the word "ausweichen" in German with S3 (a female from Germany) and S1 (a female from Poland), such as "change" "swerve" "squeeze" and "omit". As indicated in the transcribed conversation, the word "ausweichen" means "swerve" in English, the three non-native speakers in this conversation have already found the exact word, but they fail to pick it out. However, although these non-native speakers does not get the exact corresponding word to the German word "ausweichen" in this conversation, they all have no difficulty in understanding what S2 is trying to convey. In this case, the English word "omit" has been endowed with the meaning of "swerve". Therefore, in communication where situated non-native speakers are involved, they tend to endow new meanings to the existing word through mutual cooperation so as to get communication through.

Using an alternative word including synonyms, near synonyms, hyponyms and even words beyond that is regarded as a form of pragmatic creativity. For non-native speakers, not only do they have to overcome unsystematic grammar in spoken communication, but the limited vocabulary is also an obstacle for them. Under such circumstance, non-native speakers apply pragmatic creativity in lexical forms, such as using an alternative word. In most cases, the word used is related to the conventional one in the very context. Thus, with the cooperation of other interlocutors who are present, it is possible for situated interlocutors to get communication through by producing alternative words, a form of pragmatic creativity.

#### 4.2.2.3 Describing an Intended Word

For non-native speakers, it is often the case that a word is not within reach when inneed due to the limited vocabulary as well as low usage. In this case, other than using alternative words, describing a word is another form of pragmatic creativity in lexicon that non-native speakers will apply. Similar to the form of using an alternative word, describing an intended word will also apply synonyms, near synonyms as well as hyponyms to getting the communication through. The different point lies in that when non-native speakers are describing a word, they do not just make a compromise, such as using synonyms, near synonyms or hyponyms, they also offer specific explanations.

Notional words, such as nouns and verbs, are frequently described in communication.

(4.21) V: So, time in that planet travels much slower than time in the earth.

L: Oh.

V: When they come back to the, what call that, the, the, thing they on it.

L: The rocket.

V: Somekind, the rocket?

L: Ye.

V: *Not only the rocket, the thing sent by the rocket, but . . .*

L: Ahum.

S: Astronaut.

V: *Astronaut? Astronaut is people, not people, just the space.*

L: Oh.

V: *Like the room they send to the space?*

L: Oh.
V: The space station?
L: Yes.
V: Ye, and when they went back to that station, it's like 23 years later, so . . .
L: Oh my heaven-ness.

In this conversation, V (a woman from China) is sharing the story of the film *Interstellar* with others (L is a female from the US and S is a male from Burma.). However, when she is telling other interlocutors about the space station, she gets stuck. Therefore, she tries to ask other interlocutors who are present for help. There are several ways that V describes the word. For example, she first says "what call that, the, the, thing they on it", which indicates the usage of the object, and then "not only the rocket, the thing sent by the rocket, but", which indicates how the object is related to other things, and finally "astronaut is people, not people, just the space", which indicates the attribute of the object. Through clarifying her description of the word, she tries to find out the word step by step. Finally, with the help of other interlocutors, she gets the word, which is confirmed by others. In describing a noun, details about the word is usually given, such as its usage, attribute as well as relationship with other things that the non-native speaker knows in their conversation, so as to lead other interlocutors to get the word she is trying to offer. In forms of pragmatic creativity like this, mutual cooperation of situated interlocutors is of vital importance in communication.

Similar cases can also be found in our data. In the following piece of conversation, instead of describing a noun, the non-native speaker S tries to describe an adjective.

(4.22) S: Which country yoga come from China or India? Which country is come from?
V: India.

S：India，or China?

L：India，I think of yoga.

S：This is what kind of?

L：What kind of yoga?

S：Ye，ye，it's meditate，*or it's for*，*for the body*，*skinly*，or mentally.

I：Physical.

S：Physically.

I：Yes.

In this conversation，S（a man from Burma），V（a woman from China），L（a woman from America）and I（a woman from India）are discussing about the origin of yoga and the type of yoga in India. When S mentions the types of yoga in India，he is confused about the two main classifications，one is mental，and the other is physical. However，when it comes to the description of the physical type of yoga，S feels it a little difficult to find the specific word to describe the situation. Therefore，he applies different expressions，such as "for the body" and "skinly"，though none of which fits the one that he is describing. As an India origin，speaker I seems to know more about yoga，and corrects what S says by providing the exact word "physical" to help communication through. S，who repeats the word to confirm its usage，also accepts this word. While describing the word "physical"，there are two things that S provides in working out with I. For one thing，it's the attribute or meaning of this word. For another，S also tries to pair the word he is looking for with the word "mentally". During this process，he also describes the corresponding attribute of the mental type of yoga，to "meditate". Through the two aspects，it makes it easier for other interlocutors to provide what the non-native speaker is looking for. Both context and mutual cooperation among interlocutors help to achieve non-native speakers' successful communication，the process of which is the interplay of non-native speakers' attention and intention as suggested in the socio-cognitive approach.

Describing a word seems easy; however, it also requires some techniques. As we have mentioned above, the word that non-native speakers describe is usually a notional word. Second, some basic information about the wordwill be provided based on the context, such as the word's attribute, usage and so on. Finally, relationship with other related objects or topics in conversations might also be given, such as comparison, dependence and attachment. Non-native speakers creatively use all forms of pragmatic creativity, including finding the intended word, to help communication go smoothly through cooperating with other interlocutors who are present in the conversational context. In this way, expressions in conversations are creatively equipped with a new denotation at the discourse level.

#### 4.2.2.4 Creating a New Word

Creating a new word is not as frequent as other lexical forms of pragmatic creativity in non-native speakers in communication as indicated in our data, since it requires the speaker to follow some word formation rules, or else, the word created won't be easy for other interlocutors to understand. There are two reasons for this. In our data analysis, all the forms of pragmatic creativity are applied to help communication go through instead of creating certain communicative effect, for instance humor or irony. Thus, pragmatic creativity for achieving certain communicative effects does not belong to our analysis scope. On the other hand, words created without following certain rules would cause some confusion in understanding as mentioned above, and thus, non-native speakers, who are of comparatively low language proficiency, would not adopt this form.

In spite of these reasons, some non-native speakers, who are familiar with some word-formation rules, try to create new words to help their communication go through. Here is the example.

(4.23) L: For your son, what would you tell him to look for in a woman, that he wanted to marry?

H: Mm, I, I, as I said, I just comment for my marriage, first of all, it is important thing of, first of all, we put on a thing is personality.

L: Is?

H: Personality.

L: Personality. Yes.

H: And sincerely, and diligent.

L: And intelligent?

H: Ye.

L: Nice.

H: Kind.

L: Kindness.

H: Kindness, or nice, and also endurance, and . . .

L: Yes.

H: Sacripile? Sacripile? Sacripile?

L: Yes?

H: *Sacrification*? *Sacrification*?

L: I am not getting that, sacri?

H: *Sacrification for family*.

L: Oh, qualifications for family?

H: Sacripile, sacripile?

V: Is that responsibility?

H: No, it's a kind of responsibility.

L: Oh, responsibility?

H: Er, I mean er, sorry, my pronunciation is not very . . .

V: Sacrifice?

H: *Sacrification*?

V: Sacrification?

H: *Sacrification for family*.

L: Yes, ok, yes, yes.

H: It is really important thing.

L: Yes, yes.

H: I think that is the personality of someone.

In this conversation, L (a woman from America) is asking H (a woman from Korea) how she will ask her son to value a woman. H lists several characteristics of a person, such as being sincere, diligent, kind, nice, enduring, etc. However, when she mentions that a woman needs to sacrifice for her family, H has trouble in making it clear. Based on the partial pronunciation, we can tell that she knows a word that meets her need, but she can't remember it clearly or pronounce it in an understandable way. As a result, it causes the confusion for the rest of interlocutors. Based on her pronunciation, others may not guess what she is saying either (other interlocutors in the conversation try to guess "qualification for family" and "is that a kind of responsibility"). All the efforts do not seem to work until V (a woman from China) comes up with the word "sacrifice". It is not until then that the rest of the interlocutors get to understand the word "sacrification" that H keeps saying. As we know, the word "sacrifice" is both a verb and a noun, and there is not such a noun form for the word "sacrifice" as "sacrification". Despite the inexistence of such a word, all the interlocutors accept her way of using this word. This is because the word "sacrification" in H's sense has been assigned with a temporary new meaning by mutual cooperation and situated interlocutors. It has been taken as a noun form of "sacrifice" instead of being treated as a wrong use or being misunderstood by other interlocutors. In this case, H has overgeneralized the word formation rule of changing a verb to its corresponding noun form. After figuring out the pronunciation, other interlocutors accept the word and successful communication is achieved.

Similar cases are not rare, in which non-native speakers try to create new words to help communication go through smoothly.

(4.24) A: Dear X, you are so good at chopsticks. Great!

X: Thank you, I think I am.

B: How long did it take you to learn to use chopsticks?

X: En, it might not be very long. You know now in Australia, many young people are used to using chopsticks.

C: Wow, really?

X: Yes, it is true. Chinese culture is good, they like to learn.

A: How many times have you been to China before?

X: How many times? I am not sure, but I came to China almost every year since 1994.

A: Wow, You have been through to China for 21 years! Then you must be a, how to say, er, Mr. Know All. No, en . . .

C: *En, u u . . . Mr. Chinese. You are a Mr. Chinese!*

All: . . .

X: Ah, ha ha. I hope I am, and there are still many things for me to learn.

In this conversation, some Chinese scholars are having dinner with X, who is a scholar from Australia. They are chatting casually before they find that the Australian scholar has been to China frequently in the past 20 years. One of the Chinese, A, intends to say that X must be a China hand, which means someone who is very familiar with all kinds of cultural traditions in China. However, he is stuck in finding the exact word to express what he intends to. Under that circumstance, speaker C, who gets A's intention, creatively provides the expression "Mr. Chinese". As a hearer, speaker C catches speaker A's intention based on his utterance and the immediate context. While as a speaker as well as a hearer, C tries to figure out how to express the exact meaning based on his own language ability. Although there is not such an expression called "Mr. Chinese", it does not prevent other speakers in the conversation from getting what speaker A and C are trying to convey. Thus, in this case, the expression "Mr. Chinese" is creatively given a new meaning as "China hand" for the time being based on mutual cooperation of interlocutors who are at presence.

Creating a new word is a form of pragmatic creativity which is not frequently adopted by non-native speakers in communication, since it requires one to know about some word formation rules as we mentioned at the beginning of this section. As illustrated in previous cases, non-native speakers tend to create words or expressions that do not necessarily exist in the target language system. In the previous chapter, it has been pointed out that pragmatic creativity in non-native speakers' communication is a situated term instead of a systematic one, thus the context, especially the immediate context is of vital importance to understand the form of pragmatic creativity. Besides, it helps to prove that pragmatic creativity is a linguistic phenomenon that is achieved at the discourse level instead of the utterance level.

### 4.2.3 Pragmatic Creativity in Collocation Deviation

Collocation is always taken as an innovative way in communication, not only in native speakers' communication, but also in non-native speakers'. For Cogo and Dewey (2012: 70), how "the words are combined to form collocations and fixed expressions" is creative for non-native speakers. Based on their corpus, they distinguish the distribution of different types of collocations in ELF and ENL. While for Prodromou (2008: 222), creativity in collocation involves the variation between L1 version and L2 version. For example, the general expression for L1 is to "raise an eyebrow" and "pre-empt problems", while for L2, the version is to "lift an eyebrow" and "waylay problems". The focus of creativity in collocation for Cogo and Dewey, and Prodromou lies in the difference between L1 and L2 speakers. In addition, preposition is viewed as an isolated part in creativity. However, in our discussion, this is a different case. Firstly, the focus of our discussion is how non-native speakers use creative collocation, which is taken as a form of pragmatic creativity, to help them get communication through. Secondly, preposition is also believed to fall into the scope of collocation in this book. In the following sections, with the analytical method of the socio-cognitive approach, our discussion will mainly center on two points.

#### 4.2.3.1 Deviating Prepositional Phrases in Collocation

As mentioned at the beginning of this section, studies of preposition in non-native speakers' communication is not a rare thing. Generally speaking, there are mainly three types of propositional collocations in non-native speakers' communication. First of all, there is the omission of prepositions, such as lack of the preposition "at" in the expression "look at" and "to" in the expression "listen to". Secondly, there is the addition of prepositions. For example, an extra preposition "to" may be added to expressions of "go home". Last but not least, there is the alternation of L1 preferred way of using prepositions. For non-native speakers, it's a common problem that they may be confused about whether they should use a preposition or not or which preposition they should use. The omission and addition of prepositions are related to the shift of lexical functions, such as shifting a transitive verb to an intransitive verb or vice versa, as we have discussed in the previous section. Therefore, in our discussion, we will mainly focus on the last type of preposition use.

In communication where non-native speakers are involved, they do not always use preposition in the same way as native speakers do due to their limited language proficiency. Under that circumstance, creative use of preposition occurs in their communication in order to avoid communicative problems.

(4.25) Y: L, do you remember the artist, he took the photos I bringed last year, he is dead.

H: Oh my god.

L: Oh dear, what happened to him?

H: Yesterday, last night, *I saw in TV*, he killed himself at home, nobody knows what happened.

L: Oh, how sad, he is such a great artist. I like the pictures you brought.

Y: Ye. Some people say he is killed by the government, but, no one knows what really happened.

In the above example, Y (a female from Korea) is sharing a piece of sad news with H (another female from Korea) and L (a female from the US). Hearing the sad news, L is curious about what has happened to the artist. Thus, Y offers the source of the information as well as more details of the artist's death. While sharing the information, Y uses the collocation "in TV" instead of "on TV", which is considered as the more appropriate expression to convey what Y intends to. The difference between the two expressions is that the former generally refers to the TV station as a work unit, while the latter means TV programs, like TV shows or news reports and so on. In this conversation, although Y's creative collocation of the preposition "in" with TV does not match what she intends to convey, it does not cause any misunderstanding or confusion in other interlocutors present as well. In this case, "in TV" is what we mean by the collocation form of pragmatic creativity in non-native speakers' communication. Although it is grammatically correct at the sentence level, it is inappropriate at the utterance level. However, if we take a look at the discourse level, through the cooperation with other interlocutors who are present, we can see that they totally understand what this expression means in this case. The collocation form of pragmatic creativity is based on its conversational context, mutual cooperation of interlocutors as well as their prior and actual situational experience.

Not all novel collocations of prepositions are forms of pragmatic creativity, but only those accepted by other interlocutors in communication. Pragmatic creativity is a term in the situational sense instead of the systematic sense. It will be much easier for us to know more about the situational feature of pragmatic creativity if we compare the following case with the example (4.25).

(4.26) J: Have you ever rowed a boat before?

All: No.

L: But we have the experience of boating, you know, but just sitting there.

J: Oh, you have the experience of boating?

L: No, but I see that in TV.

J: In TV?

L: Ye, I saw people rowing a boat in TV.

J: What does it mean by in TV?

L: Watching people boating from TV?

J: Oh, on TV?

L: Ye, on TV.

J: Oh, ok, I was thinking how could people get in TV.

L: . . .

In this conversation, L (a woman from China) is having a conversation with J (a man from America) by the boat rental office. J is asking whether others have ever had the experience of boating, and L's answer to his question is no, but she has seen others boating on TV. The phrase that L uses in the conversation is "in TV" instead of "on TV", which confuses J. Therefore, unlike the example above, J poses a question. Not getting a satisfactory answer from L, J puts the question in a more specific way and finally understands what L is trying to convey. After that, J helps correct the expression with "on TV" which makes both parties clear. In this case, although the non-native speaker L collocates the preposition "in" with "TV" in the same way as Y does in the earlier example, their communication to some degree is achieved through mutual cooperation. Nevertheless, L and J in this case work out the communication differently due to the misunderstanding that occurred, and the native speaker has to point out the inappropriate expression and correct it.

Preposition collocations that are used in a pragmatically creative way are not rare in non-native speakers' communication. We are not going to list all the situations in an infinite way but give some examples for illustration.

(4.27) L: Are you beginning to get ready for Christmas?

M: Christmas? Not yet.

L: Not yet.

V: Haha.

M: Not yet, yes. I don't know. Haha. *That's really difficult to me. It's different to my country and here, right?*

V: Haha.

Me: You know that, right?

V: Ye.

In the above conversation, L (a female from the US) is asking M (a mother from Korea) whether she has got prepared for the coming Christmas. M's answer is negative, and she also shows that Christmas has troubled her a lot. In her opinion, this is related to the cultural differences. When conveying such an idea,

M uses the preposition "to" after the adjective "difficult". However, the whole picture of the sentence is "that's really difficult to me", in which a pronoun follows the preposition "to" instead of a verb. While conveying the differences between her own culture and the culture in the US, she says "it's different to my country and here", in which the appropriate preposition should be "from" instead of "to". While for mistakes or inappropriate uses of preposition in this conversation, both the native speaker L and the non-native speaker V (a female from China) show their mutual understanding on what M intends to express. Although these two prepositions used in this piece of conversation by M are not conventional, commonly used or a native-preferred way of prepositional collocation, there is no pragmatic misunderstanding aroused in the context, and it is interlocutors' recognition of M's intention that helps communication go through.

Pragmatic creativity shown in the form of collocation of preposition is common. However, as we have mentioned above, if we only look at the collocation of preposition at the sentence or utterance level, the sentence or utterance is unacceptable, even at the sentence level. If we switch to the discourse level, it may not be difficult for us to understand what non-native speakers intend to convey. Viewed from the socio-cognitive approach, interlocutors, whether native speakers or non-native speakers, are egocentric in communication. That is to say, non-native speakers may be influenced by their low language proficiency as well as their mother tongue. Prepositional phrases, which do not carry so much meanings as notional words do in the target language, may vary a lot from non-native speakers' first language, and it is thus understandable when they switch the collocation from one preposition to another.

### 4.2.3.2 Deviating Verbal Phrases in Collocation

Similar to the collocation of prepositions, pragmatic creativity is also in the form of collocation of verbal phrases in non-native speakers' communication, in which way they may break the fixed phrases and recombine with parts from other phrases or add some other words so as to meet their conversational needs. Besides, there are also situations in which non-native speakers choose parts of a phrase and use it as a whole to convey their intended meaning.

Some partial phrases that non-native speakers apply are from two or more phrases. These phrases, to some degree, are synonymic phrases. Others are just newly created phrases based on the specific one that should have been used in the context. The following is an example in which non-native speakers decollate two or more phrases and recombine them as a new one.

(4.28) A: You know, last time I went fishing with some locals, and they just catch and let free.
B: Ye, they just let free!
C: Catch and release?
A: Ye, release.

In this example, A (a woman from China) is sharing her fishing experience with B (a woman from China) and C (a man from America). When A is talking about her experience, B agrees with A that it is not usual for someone who catches the fish and releases it. In this conversation, both A and B accept the way they recombine the phrase "let free". Based on their common ground about fishing and the immediate context, C, who is a native English speaker, infers that what A intends to express is "release" instead of "let free". For native speaker C, there is not a phrase as "let free", but he tries to make it meaningful at the discourse level. While for non-native speaker A, "let free" has been privatized the same as the phrase "set free" or "let go" which literally means "release". However, what A actually does is combining a part of the phrase "let go" with a part of the phrase "set free", and thus, the newly collocated phrase turns out to be "let free". As for B, who is also a non-native speaker with low language proficiency, does not realize any inappropriateness with the phrase. The personal factors, such as language proficiency and different social-cultural backgrounds, increase non-native speakers' tolerance of unconventional collocations. While for C, a native speaker, he can quickly respond to the unfamiliar or unconventional collocation of the phrase. In spite of that, both B and C get the point that A is transmitting in the specific context. The collocation in this context is understood as a form of pragmatic creativity for non-native speakers. With the socio-cognitive approach, it is easier for us to know how such kind of inappropriate expression can help communication go through.

Non-native speakers not only separate and recombine phrases, but also use a part of a whole phrase as a complete one in communication.

(4.29) M: It's always the same thing, I am doing the same.

V: Maybe tell us something about your children, haha.

M: My children? Haha.

V: Lots of to say, right?

M: I am a bad mum for them, *I didn't care of them*.

V: Haha.

L: You are not a bad mama, I know.

The above conversation is among M (a mother from Korea), V (a female from China) and L (a female from the US). In this conversation, M is a little depressed and she is complaining about her tedious life. Noticing that, V encourages M to share the trouble concerning her own children. However, M does not seem to be in the mood of talking about her children, and she claims herself as a "bad" mother, and accuses herself of not having taken good care of the children. However, when expressing the meaning of "take care of", M did not manage to use the conventional phrase but just a part of it, which is "care of". In the phrase "take care of", the word "care" undertakes the major meaning of the phrase. As a non-native speaker of low language proficiency, M is not capable of manipulating the target language fluently, especially phrases. Therefore, in this case, she adopts the main part of the phrase but drops the verb, which semantically does not have any meaning. As pointed out in the previous chapter, for non-native speakers of low language proficiency, pragmatics is almost equal to semantics. Therefore, in this case, the non-native speaker M creatively uses a part of the phrase to express what she intends to say in communication, and the other two interlocutors who are present get what she is conveying without difficulty. The context together with mutual cooperation of the situated interlocutors helps to get communication through.

Combining verbs with other nouns, prepositions and/or other elements to form a verbal phrase is one of the linguistic phenomena in English. Thus, for non-native speakers, it is common that they mix verbal phrases. What these non-native speakers do in communication is to create a new verbal phrase or to split an old one to form a new one through various ways, such as spliting two verbal phrases or using a part of the whole phrase as shown in the examples above. Egocentric non-native speakers may apply other ways when they deviate verbal phrases. In spite of that, interlocutors involved will try their best to work out and get the communication through, which is based on the immediate context through mutual cooperation.

#### 4.2.3.3 Deviating Formulaic Expressions in Collocation

Formulaic expressions cover a wide range of expressions, such as idioms, sayings, proverbs and fixed metaphors, and some may also involve fixed verbal phrases as mentioned above. Formulaic expressions refer to "multiword collocations that are stored and retrieved holistically rather than being generated de novo with each use" (Kecskes, 2013a: 105). Based on previous studies, Wray (2013: 317) puts forward that the "formulaic language" is "sequence(s) of words that is (are) in some regard not entirely predictable, whether on account of a meaning that is wildly or subtly different from the words they contain, a function that is only achieved with the whole expression, or features of structure such as morphology or word order that are non-canonical". According to previous studies, formulaic language is used as a whole and seldom used in separation. For non-native speakers, to apply formulaic language incommunication is usually creative since they are trying to act in a native-like way. However, pragmatic creativity is also built in a different way when such kind of expressions are involved in communication. Although formulaic expressions also include some fixed verbal phrases, in the following discussion, we will mainly focus on other formulaic expressions.

In the previous two sections, we have discussed that non-native speakers tend to deviate both propositional and verbal phrases in communication. The unintentional and deliberate behavior employed by non-native speakers in communication is to make interlocutors understand or to keep communication going through smoothly. The following case shows how it works.

(4.30) S: *How did you today*?

L: Ye, good, good to see you.

S: Thank you.

L: Very good, um, ok, er . . .

V: And also last week, S just sent me to my home, ye.

L: Oh he took you home.

V: Ye.

L: Last week.

V: Last week.

S: Ye, we are.

L: Thank you.

This conversation is among S (a male from Burma), L (a female from the US) and V (a female from China). Before the conversation, all the interlocutors are in a chatting room, this conversation begins as S walks into the room. S first greets L, and then V shares some information with L about what S did the week before. Upon entering the room, S greets L by uttering "How did you today?" and Lresponds with "Ye, good, good to see you." Generally speaking, people usually say "How are you?" or "How are you today?" to greet others. However, in this case, S does not seem to get the right formulaic expression. What he can recall is the structure of a interrogative sentence. In addition, the time when they meet is early evening, and it seems for S that using the word "how" is a serious way of asking others about their life during the day. All these reasons combined lead to S's unique way of deviating the formulaic expression of greeting. According to the timing when S utters the sentence, there is no difficulty for L to find out what S intends to convey. As a non-native speaker, S has already done his best to make him/herself understood, while L and V also try their best to get what S is trying to convey based on the context and their knowledge that S is a foreigner of low English proficiency. Therefore, the conversational context together with the mutual cooperation among interlocutors helps non-native speakers' unconventional formulaic expression find its way out in communication.

The following case is the one that we have mentioned in the previous chapter. Here it can be used again as a case to exemplify how the non-native speakers deviates the formulaic expression.

(4.31) Sophie: Hey, every body! *It's raining cats and goats out there.*

Caroline: Didn't you mean "cats and dogs"?

Sophie: Oh, it's so nice to be corrected as you walk in the door.

(*Two Broke Girls*, Season IV, Episode 10)

In this sitcom, the relationship between Sophie (a female from Poland) and Caroline (a female from the US) are neighbors. Caroline is a waitress in the restaurant, and the conversation happens when Sophie drops by to visit her boyfriend who works in the same restaurant with Caroline. In the conversation, Sophie creatively substitutes "goats" for "dogs" in using the idiom "it's raining cats and dogs" which means it's raining heavily. As a native speaker, Caroline connects what Sophie said with the salientidiom structure "it's raining cats and dogs" in English quickly. Based on the actual situation that Sophie is coming with an umbrella, Caroline has no difficulty figuring out what Sophie intends to convey. While Caroline, a native speaker, naturally notices it is not a conventional phrase or formulaic expression. However, Sophie, who makes a mistake in using the idiom, doesn't seem to care about that problem. This also explains why it is so important to discuss pragmatic creativity in non-native speakers' communication. In this case, Sophie would have used the original idiom, since her intention is to get communication through and transmit the information about the weather, but she unintentionally produces a creative form. Besides, it doesn't prevent Sophie from making her communicative intention clear. Even though she is confused about the type of animal that should be used in the idiom, which may be related to etymology, her audience still gets what she tries to convey. Therefore, viewed from the socio-cognitive approach, in its conversational context, the deviated collocation of pragmatic creativity helps to get communication through by situated interlocutor's mutual cooperation and their personal experience and knowledge.

Besides deviating a part of the formulaic expression, there are other cases in which non-native speakers use completely new expressions functioning as formulaic expressions so as to achieve their communicative intention.

(4.32) S: So how are you getting along with your life here?

C: Thank you, en, you know it seems everything goes well with my Ph.D. book writing.

S: That's good to know, what are you going to do when you finish your book?

C: En, you know, that's what I would like to ask for your help. It seems I have got too much idea and is wondering about what to do exactly.

S: It's quite normal for one to have too much idea at one time.

C: Yes, I really want to do many things at one time, so I am puzzled.

S: You said it, but you can only have one focus.

C: Yes, I know. *It is something like a greedy snake that wants to swallow down an elephant.*

S: Ah, I see. That's interesting.

C: Do you have similar sayings?

S: Yes, we say, our eyes are bigger than our bellies. But yours is a very interesting and vivid one.

This conversation takes place between a Chinese scholar C (male) and an Australian scholar S (female). C is talking to S that he wants to do a lot of things at the same time but is puzzled by how he can manage them. S agrees with him. Thus C produces a saying originated from Chinese, "It is something like a greedy snake that wants to swallow down an elephant". Despite the fact that some encyclopedic knowledge and culturally-preferred way are contained in the English version of the Chinese saying, S does not seem to misunderstand or get confused with what C says based on the immediate context. She even provides with a corresponding one in English. As an egocentric non-native speaker, C does not necessarily know the original English saying, and thus he tries to use a Chinese saying to express his understanding of "greedy". Therefore, he creates the new saying on the linguistic encyclopedic knowledge of his first language, Chinese. Based on their mutual cooperation, it does not take much effort to work out what C is saying. Although the saying has been literally translated into the target language, as an unconventional expression, it still helps C to get their communication through.

Low language proficiency is one of the reasons why non-native speakers deviate formulaic expressions in collocation, but it is not a definite one. As pointed out at the beginning of this section, formulaic expressions involve not only fixed verbal phrases, but also idioms, sayings, proverbs as well as frozen metaphors and situation-bound utterances. Therefore, non-native speakers of comparatively higher languageproficiency may be confused with some formulaic expressions. Such is the case in example (4.32). Deviating formulaic expressions in collocation is one of the forms of pragmatic creativity in non-native speakers' communication. It seems that breaking the original structure, substituting one or more words in the formulaic expression with another or even translating formulaic expression of one's native language into the target language all turn out to be an efficient way for non-native speakers to achieve successful communication.

## 4.3 Reasons for Non-native Speakers to Be Pragmatically Creative

Pragmatic creativity in non-native speakers' communication is mainly concerned with creative uses of language. For native speakers, to be creative is to achieve certain communicative effects, such as humor, sarcasm, insinuation and so on. While for non-native speakers, pragmatics is almost equal to semantics (Kecskes, 2013a: 121), especially for novice. Therefore, the main purpose that non-native speakers display pragmatic creativity in their utterances is to perform the function as required in the communication process. In this section, we will look into the reasons for pragmatic creativity in non-native speakers' communication.

### 4.3.1 Communicative Needs

The main issue that non-native speakers are concerned about is to "achieve shared understanding and successful communicative outcomes" (Kaur, 2011: 113) or to focus on "interpersonal and individual concern" (House, 1999: 84). The main purpose for non-native speakers to be pragmatically creative is known as to achieve successful communication, in which different forms of pragmatic creativity are used to meet different communicative needs in communication.

Meeting the communicative needs is regarded as the very first reason for non-native speakers to apply pragmatic creativity. If there is no pragmatic creativity in communication, non-native speakers tend to produce unaccepted forms or even zero form (silence) in their communication, which would lead to failed communication. The chart below illustrates this relationship:

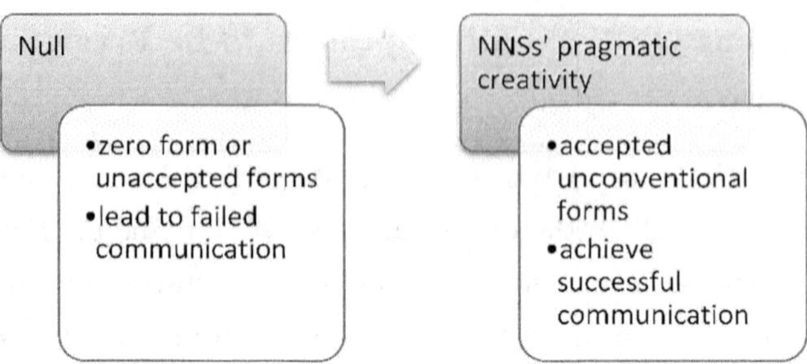


**Chart 2. Reasons for non-native speakers to be pragmatically creative in communication**

According to this chart, non-native speakers may produce zero form (keep silent) or produce unacceptable utterances to other interlocutors in the very context, and either will lead to failed communication. However, non-native speakers' utterances that display pragmatic creativity will help them achieve successful communication. Cultural information or knowledge is implied in language, while language is a social cultural resource (Bondi, 2007: 54) constituted by "a range of possibilities" (Halliday, 1973: 49). For native speakers, cultural information has been encoded in their language, and no extra efforts are needed in their communication. However, this is not the same case for non-native speakers. Non-native speakers usually have less cultural background information of the target language, and they are of relatively low language proficiency Pragmatic creativity is thus motivated by communicative needs in non-native speakers' communication.

In a word, non-native speakers'pragmatic creativity arises as successful communication requires.

### 4.3.2 Positive Cooperative Attitude

Grice (1975: 45) defines Cooperative Principle as "make your conversational contribution such as is required, at the stage at which it occurs, by the accepted purpose or direction of the talk exchange in which you are engaged". Lots of scholars try to divide "cooperation" as defined by Grice into several subcategories, such as "social" "linguistic/formal" cooperation (Lumsden, 2008) and so on. One of the examples that Grice's theory is flawed summarized by Hadi (2013: 71) is that Grice ignores people may "intentionally miscommunicate" sometimes. However, the kind of cooperation that Grice refers to is an instinctive one instead of cooperation in a concrete form. In language communication, cooperation that Grice talks about is a kind of human instinct, and so is egocentrism mentioned by Kecskes (2013a) in the socio-cognitive approach. In this sense, interlocutors are always cooperative and egocentric, no matter whether they are native speakers or non-native speakers.

Although the notion "cooperation" given by Grice is sometimes misunderstood, it doesn't mean cooperation is only instinctive. Cooperation is also intended, especially in non-native speakers' communication. Intended cooperation does not mean that interlocutors hold positive attitudes toward others' opinion, but means to keep positive cooperative attitudes in communication. We can take a look at the following example,

(4.33) S: Which country yoga come from China or India? Which country is come from?

V: India

S: India, or China?

L: India, I think of yoga.

S: This is what kind of?

L: What kind of yoga?

S: Ye, ye, it's meditate, *or it's for, for the body, skinly*, or mentally.

I: Physical.

S：Physically.

I：Yes.

In this conversation, in order to make clear what he intends to convey, S actively uses different novel forms to refer to the "physical" kind of yoga in India. S's positive cooperative attitude prompts him to display pragmatic creativity so as to proceed the conversation and help others understand easily.

Non-native speakers' linguistic and contextual resources are limited, while positive cooperative attitude leads to the pragmatic creativity in their conversation. While in native speakers' communication (mainly refers to fluent native speaker excluding baby language learners and people who have language deficiency), the positive cooperative attitude is not necessary. In understanding non-native speakers' pragmatic creativity, more efforts are required so as to get their communicative intention across, or in other words, make communication carry on successfully. Therefore, for native speakers, cooperation is usually instinctive in communication; while for non-native speakers, cooperation means to be both instinctive and positive.

### 4.3.3 Imperfect Lingual-situational Matching Efforts

Generally speaking, non-native speakers are of lower language proficiency in the target language than native speakers. Even for those non-native speakers whose language proficiency is evaluated as advanced, it is not always easy to use their limited linguistic and cultural knowledge of the target language as required in the situational context. Despite their deficiency in language proficiency, non-native speakers tend to make imperfect lingual-situational matching efforts to meet the communicative needs, that is to prevent their communication from failing.

The imperfect lingual-situational matching effort refers to

how a non-native speaker uses his/her growing yet imperfect linguistic and cultural knowledge of the target language to match with what is required in the situational context. It is also regarded as one of the reasons that non-native speakers are pragmatically creative in communication.

It usually takes time for a language to develop "from protolanguage to grammatical language" (Tin, 2011: 217), and so is the process for non-native speakers to acquire a second or foreign language. However, non-native speakers' limited linguistic resources may prevent them from uttering as native speakers do in that context. Only by making imperfect lingual-situational matching efforts can non-native speakers develop their language proficiency as native-like. In order to meet the needs as required in the communication process, non-native speakers tend to make imperfect lingual-situational matching efforts. It is during this process that pragmatic creativity appears. For example:

(4.34) V: Do you want to give her a surprise?

F: Yes, I will give her a big big shock.

L: What do you mean?

F: 大，大的大的那种放圣诞礼物的，叫什么，那种。

V: Stocking.

F: Stocking.

L: Oh, santa clause?

V: Stocking.

L: Oh, the stocking.

F: Stocking. 就是那个吗?

V: 就是那个大的袜子。

F: Yes, stocking.

L: Yes.

F: My daughter told me, maybe last week, mum, will you give me a Christmas gift? The stocking.

L: Stocking.

F：When I am sleeping.

Others：Hahaha.

F：The next day，I will surprised.

L：She sees enough TV.

Others：Hahaha.

L：Her friends，because many children，believes.

V：There is santa clause.

The above conversation is a group discussion about Christmas rituals for children. V (a woman from China) is asking whether F (a woman from China) will give a Christmas gift to her 11-year-old daughter，and F offers a positive answer. Moreover，F also says that she will give her a big "shock" which confuses L (a woman from America). Under this circumstance，F applies L1 to negotiate with V. Getting what F is describing，V provides the word "stocking". In the above conversation，"F's" linguistic resource about Christmas does not match with what she wants to convey under that circumstance. However，her growing yet imperfect lingual-situational collocation does not prevent her from transmitting what she intends to. F uses the word "shock" to express the meaning of "stocking"，which helps her follow up the conversation.

Finding a native or idiomatic way is always not easy for non-native speakers. Under that circumstance，they have to make imperfect lingual-situational matching efforts. Their limited linguistic knowledge and contextual resources promote pragmatic creativity at the discourse level with the cooperation of other interlocutors.

Pragmatic creativity is not a unique term in non-native speakers' communication. The point is that unlike pragmatic creativity in native speakers' communication，the main purpose for non-native speakers to be pragmatically creative is to get communication through. Besides, pragmatic creativity for native speakers is generally taken as an intended behavior, while for non-native speakers it is an unintentional but deliberate one. In this chapter, we mainly focus on forms of pragmatic creativity in non-native speakers' communication.

For one thing, this book on non-native speakers' communication from pragmatic creativity is chiefly analyzed from the perspective of the socio-cognitive approach with data analysis. The analysis from the socio-cognitive approach with a large amount of data collected from real situations makes it a valuable research in the field of pragmatic study. Definitions about what are termed as non-native speakers' successful communication and failed communication are given. For another, we focus on the forms of pragmatic creativity in successful ones. There are three major forms of pragmatic creativity in non-native speakers' communication. The three forms are all concerned with verbal behavior, since nonverbal behavior is not a story to tell in this book. It covers pragmatic creativity in the grammatical aspect, in lexical forms, and by deviating collocation. Pragmatic creativity in grammatical aspects includes changing utterance structures and omitting lexico-grammatical features. Pragmatic creativity in lexical forms covers shifting lexical function, using an alternative word, describing an intended word and creating a new word. Pragmatic creativity in the form of collocation involves deviating prepositional and verbal phrases and formulaic expressions.

For native speakers and non-native speakers who are creative in communication, they have different motivations. Being pragmatically creative, native speakers aim at achieving certain communicative goals. While for non-native speakers, applying pragmatic creativity often means working out a way to successful communication. The motivations or reasons for non-native speakers to be pragmatically creative are firstly to meet communicative needs in conversations with non-native speakers' positive cooperative attitude through their imperfect lingual-situational matching efforts in communication.

In a word, the analysis draws a conclusion that for non-native speakers to achieve successful communication, pragmatic creativity plays an important role.

# Chapter Five  Conclusion

Pragmatic creativity is a ready-made term, but it is a newconcept in the study of non-native speakers' communication. It is ready-made in the sense that it is not the first time the term has been put forward in the linguistic field. Gumperz (Prevignano et al., 2003) and Paradis (2009) both have briefly discussed this notion from their own perspectives. It is new because no one, as far as we know, has explored this term from the socio-cognitive approach as this book does. How we understand and conceptualize this notion for this study turns out to be the first task of this book. Previous studies have emphasized the role of context in understanding pragmatic creativity. With the guidance of the socio-cognitive approach, it is not only the context, but also interlocutors' mutual cooperation that have been highlighted in conceptualizing pragmatic creativity.

Since the main objective of this study is to investigate how pragmatic creativity becomes salient in non-native speakers' communication, our main efforts have been devoted to collecting and analyzing the data of intercultural communication. Before touching upon this question, we will take a look back at the research questions that we raised at the beginning of this study, which will help us get closer to the objective of this study: 1) Is there pragmatic creativity in non-native speakers' communication or not? If yes, what does it refer to? 2) Why are non-native speakers pragmatically creative in their communication? 3) How does pragmatic creativity present itself in non-native speakers' communication? 4) How do we understand the way that pragmatic creativity works in non-native speakers' communication?

At the very beginning of this book, the research background and significance of this study have been made clear. Based on previous studies of language creativity, the term "pragmatic creativity" is introduced. Viewed from the socio-cognitive approach, the theoretical base of intercultural pragmatics, the term "pragmatic creativity" has been delimitated. Besides, features of pragmatic creativity are illustrated in detail. On the basis of the preliminary work, forms of pragmatic creativity in non-native speakers' communication are analyzed through its interrelation with grammatical forms, lexical forms as well as collocations. Therefore, in this very last chapter, we will generally go through the following four parts: major findings, implications and limitations of this study, and moreover, suggestions for further studies.

## 5.1 Major Findings of the Study

This book is a research focusing on pragmatic creativity in non-native speakers' communication. Previous studies lay emphases on non-native speakers' language ability, social status and differences or gap between native and non-native speakers. Even for researches on intercultural communication from the perspective of pragmatics, they concern more about certain institutional conversations, such as Miranda warning, emergency call and so on. As for how non-native speakers achieve successful communication in intercultural communication where pragmatic creativity works, few scholar has ever touched upon it so far. While for studies of language and creativity, the main focus is on linguistic creativity, in which context is not the major concern. In terms of research on creativity in non-native speakers' communication, linguists mainly focus on communication strategies adopted so as to avoid misunderstandings in communication and non-native speakers' native-like selection. Thus, the major findings of this research can be summarized as follows:

First of all, this book conceptualizes the notion of pragmatic creativity with the guidance of the socio-cognitive approach, especially pragmatic creativity in non-native speakers' communication. In this book, non-native speakers' pragmatic creativity is defined as a contextualized fact that integrates situated non-native speakers' novel inputs and other interlocutors' cooperative understanding, which aims to achieve successful communication. Pragmatic creativity in non-native speakers' communication is chiefly displayed as unconventional or uncommonly used forms/expressions that aim to achieve successful communication. In addition to the vital role of context, the interlocutors' mutual cooperation is particularly emphasized in understanding pragmatic creativity in non-native speakers' communication.

Secondly, a distinction between pragmatic creativity and linguistic creativity has been clearly made. The pragmatic creativity is differentiated from linguistic creativity in at least in three aspects: 1) Pragmatic creativity is a notion in a situational sense, while linguistic creativity is in a systematic sense. 2) The fulfillment of pragmatic creativity calls only for the acceptance of both the speaker and the hearer who are present, while realization of linguistic creativity requires the acknowledgement of social conventions. 3) Context is highly valued in pragmatic creativity but not in linguistic creativity. According to Chomsky, the essential factor of linguistic creativity is not context but the correctness of grammar. While for pragmatic creativity in this book, situational or pragmatic appropriateness rather than correctness of grammar becomes the essential element.

Thirdly, this study also highlights some features of pragmatic creativity in non-native speakers' communication. The first one is situated relevance, which calls for situational context as well as both individual and interlocutors' attention and intention. The second is flexibility, subjectivity and individuality. Social-cultural aspects are more "flexible, subjective and individual" (Kecskes, 2003: 138). Logical and social-cultural (Kecskes, 2000; 2003) aspects are required by pragmatic creativity at the discourse level. Therefore, pragmatic creativity is flexible, subjective and individual. The third aspect is effect-orientation. Pragmatic creativity in either native or non-native speakers is produced by the motivation to achieve certaincommunicative aims. The differences first lie in that more active and positive mutual cooperation is required in non-native speakers' communication. In addition, pragmatic creativity is oriented to create the intended communication effects in native speakers' communication, such as humor, satire, empathy, etc. For non-native speakers, however, the main purpose is to achieve successful communication.

Last but not least, three forms of pragmatic creativity in non-native speakers' communication have been categorized based on the data collected, namely, pragmatic creativity in grammatical forms, pragmatic creativity in lexical forms, and pragmatic creativity by deviating collocation. According to the data analysis, we conclude that pragmatic creativity in grammatical forms includes creating new sentence formats (such as using L2 preferred question structures pointed out by Prodromou (2010)), applying uncommonly used sentence structures (such as omitting auxiliary verbs or copulative verbs), using structurally unconventional sentences (such as replacing general question structures with declarative sentence structures) and so on. While for negative sentences, non-native speakers tend to use logic formula to replace the conventional or uncommonly used way of expressing negative meanings. As for pragmatic creativity in lexical forms, it includes shifting lexical function (such as "noun to verb" or "verb to noun" and "mixed use of transitive and intransitive verb"), using an "alternative word" (such as "using an alternative word" including synonyms, near synonyms, hyponyms and so on), describing an intended word (such as describing a notional word based on its attribute, usage and so on) and creating a new word (such as creating a word that does not exist). As for the forms of deviating collocation, they cover the deviation of prepositional phrases in collocation (such as changing the preposition in a fixed phrase), deviation of verbal phrases in collocation (such as mixing verbal phrases as well as words that follow the verb) and deviation of formulaic expressions in collocation (such as breaking the original structure or substituting one or more words in a formulaic expression with another).

On the whole, although some findings in this book have been very encouraging and instructive for non-native speakers' communication, it is still a very tentative endeavor that needs to be further expanded.

## 5.2 Implications of the Study

With the framework of the socio-cognitive approach, pragmatic creativity in non-native speakers' communication is a new topic in this field. This study, which aims to explore how pragmatic creativity helps non-native speakers to achieve successful communication, is a complimentary study to that of creativity in language and intercultural pragmatics. In this study, we not only apply the ready-made corpus of VOICE, but also build a complimentary corpus of intercultural communication so as to make the analysis more convincing and consolidating.

First and foremost, this research enriches the study of creativity in language, and defines the term "pragmatic creativity", especially when it is concerned with non-native speakers. In other words, creativity in language can be developed further under various definitions of this term. Studies of creativity in linguistics have been limited to the scope of generative creativity and lexical creativity since Chomsky (1964b). Later, it covers figures of speech, styles of text and so on. Pragmatic elements have also been introduced to the study of creativity in language; however, most of relevant studies are just limited to the utterance level and its functions. This study of non-native speakers' pragmatic creativity focuses on some unconventional or uncommonly used expressions or forms at the discourse level. Both discourse context and interlocutors influence the understanding of non-native speakers' utterance. The contextualized fact that situated non-native speakers using uncommon or unconventional expressions or forms so as to achieve successful communication at the discourse level is definitely not what Chomsky terms as "linguistic creativity", but "pragmatic creativity" in this argument.

Next, the study of pragmatic creativity expands the research scope of non-native speakers' communication as well as intercultural communication. Studies involving non-native speakers have turned out to be a new trend in linguistic studies, especially in intercultural communication. Preexistent studies of non-native speakers' communication that focus on misunderstandings and cultural differences are thought to be the primary reason that leads to misunderstandings. Kaur (2011: 113) has also pointed out that this may not "simply be a matter of cultural difference" but "the failure of the minority speaker to adhere to the norms, both cultural and linguistic, of the majority group". Previous studies on non-native speakers' communication put more emphasis on non-native speakers' ability as well as their social status regarding the social or cultural differences or gap between native and non-native speakers. Even for studies in the pragmatic tradition, which is concerned with intercultural communication, most of them regard certain institutional conversations, such as Miranda warning, emergency call and so on as their focuses. Less attention has been paid to how non-native speakers achieve successful communication in intercultural communication.

Third, from the perspective of pragmatic creativity, this study is also valuable with empirical implications, which are meaningful in both daily intercultural communication and second language acquisition. Most non-native speakers may feel inferior to produce any uncommonly used or unconventional sentences in communication. However, as long as what has been uttered can lead to successful communication, it is a kind of pragmatic creativity as it is helpful to make the communication continue. Uncommonly used sentence structures, vocabularies, unconventional proverbs or sayings used by non-native speakers are forms regarded as pragmatic creativity to proceed the communication. In this book, different forms of pragmatic creativity work not just as a guide for non-native speakers, but also as a theoretical and empirical instruction for non-native speakers to express their ideas by using the target language.

Last but not least, this study introduces a new perspective to the study of intercultural pragmatics.Therefore, it is indicated that intercultural pragmatics, which provides a different theoretical framework for understanding intercultural communication, should be further developed in future studies concerning intercultural factors. Theoretically speaking, intercultural pragmatics provides a theoretical foundation for this research, in which socio-cognitive approach helps us define the term "pragmatic creativity", and analyze pragmatic creativity in actual communication. Pragmatic creativity should be explained at the discourse level instead of merely at the sentence or utterance level. Non-native speakers are not only a speaker but also a hearer, who can both produce and comprehend utterances.

In sum, this study is a complementary study to previous studies of creativity in language and intercultural communication. It is of practical significance since the findings are based on actual communication, which is be meaningful and instructive for non-native speakers in daily communication. Moreover, the theoretical significance of this study lies in that it extends the development of studies of intercultural pragmatics, which functions as a basis for future studies in the field of pragmatic studies.

## 5.3 Limitations of the Study

While this study provides practical and theoretical significance for the further analysis of pragmatic creativity in non-native speakers' communication, it is also an open-ended research as most of other similar researches suggest. This study is not free from limitations:

First of all, this study is just a tentative rather than a well-grounded one in analyzing pragmatic creativity in non-native speakers' communication. Although we have defined the term "pragmatic creativity" and summarized the features of pragmatic creativity as well as the reasons for non-native speakers to be pragmatically creative in communication, pragmatic creativity in native speakers' communication hasn't been touched upon in this book. Since the research object is not within this book's concern, it is worthy of further study.

Second, some uncontrollable variables that should have been taken into account are not considered in this study due to the fact that the data is from naturally occurring conversations. The data sources are manifolds: raw recorded data from a language-learning group and ready-made online data from the corpus of VOICE. The non-native speakers from the online corpus VOICE are mostly experienced and more advanced non-native speakers, and those from the language-learning group are evaluated as advanced based on the group classification. However, there is no specific distinction between the two groups of non-native speakers. Thus, the language proficiency of non-native speakers in the data used in this book is not a fixed variable. This is due to the fact that in naturally occurring data, it is not so practical to evaluate interlocutors' language proficiency.

Last but not least, it is noticeable that certain nonverbal behavior in our data functions somehow similarly to pragmatic creativity in non-native speakers' communication. However, since it is not what we mean by pragmatic creativity, we have separated it from forms of pragmatic creativity in non-native speakers' communication. The relationship between nonverbal behavior and pragmatic creativity is also worthy of further studies.

## 5.4 Suggestions for Future Research

Generally speaking, this book is a preliminary research on how non-nativespeakers achieve successful communication with various forms of pragmatic creativity. It is not mature and is far from perfection, and much remains to be explored further. Practically speaking, creativity is an essential topic in every field. Pragmatic creativity is not the only field that should be further explored, but other interesting topics concerning creativity in language also deserve academic attention. In this book, we mainly focus on non-native speakers' pragmatic creativity, while other subjects, such as native speakers or children, are still left for further discussion. More researches related to pragmatic creativity remain to be explored further. First, the difference between pragmatic creativity and linguistic creativity is a topic worthy of further research, which we have touched upon in this research without going into details. Second, we can go further to refine and build up a well-grounded research frame of how to connect socio-cognitive approach with the illustration of non-native speakers' pragmatic creativity. Apart from that, we also suggest that a larger corpus with more accurate and controllable variables be offered in future studies. In that case, the data will be more convincing on all aspects. Though we have summarized three major forms of pragmatic creativity in non-native speakers' communication with a deep and consistent research interest in pragmatic creativity, more forms or subtypes are waiting for us to be categorized, which will be helpful to validate the present research findings.

Besides, whether pragmatic creativity has been under thorough discussion or not is still open for further discussion. The main purpose of applying pragmatic creativity by non-native speakers is to achieve successful communication, while for native speakers, pragmatic creativity tend to aim at creating certain communicative effects, such as humorous effects, sarcasm, insinuation and so on. As for the forms of pragmatic creativity of non-native speakers, only three forms are categorized, and more forms wait to be categorized. For example, nonverbal behavior used by non-native speakers during intercultural communication is also worthy of further study. As for the nonverbal forms of pragmatic creativity of native speakers, it awaits further discussion. Let's take this piece of conversation as an example:

(5.1) T: I hate mat, you know, mat, mat.
L: You hit back?
T: Mat.
V: Mat.
T: Ye.
C: What is mat? Mat?
L: Oh.
T: Ei, ye, (laughter), ye.
C: What is, what is mat?
L: Ye.
T: Mat, er . . . (writing 1+1 = 2)
C: Oh, math, math, mathematics.
L: Oh.
T: Ye, ye, ye.

In the above conversation, T (a man from Thailand) is telling others that he hates math; however, the way he pronounces the word "math" confuses others. L (a woman from America) doesn't seem to take any further step to know what T is saying, while C (a woman from China) actively asks for clarification of the word "mat" pronounced by T. Trapped in the difficult situation that no one understands his pronunciation, T tries to use mathematical expressions "1+1=2" to connect what he wants to say with the word that confuses others. This creative way of writing relevant things helps T explain what he intends to say. Such kind of unconventional nonverbal behavior also helps non-native speakers to get communication through, which functions as pragmatic creativity in the same way tosome degree. As we know, it is also possible to apply nonverbal behaviors during communication between native speakers, if they are from different dialect regions with the same first language. This is also the reason why we don't want to confuse readers with the nonverbal behaviors analysis in this book, but there are some interesting points in this, which is worthwhile for further study.

To sum up, pragmatic creativity is a new topic in the field of pragmatic study. As a topic of both theoretical and empirical significance, pragmatic creativity is worthy of further painstaking studies, since it offers some insights into how non-native speakers make their communication proceed with their low language proficiency. On the other hand, it offers strength and encouragement to those non-native speakers who are shy to speak up in similar situated contexts which leads to failed communication.

# Bibliography

[1] ANDER S, YILDIRIM Ö. Lexical errors in elementary level EFL learners' compositions[J]. Procedia — Social and Behavioral Sciences, 2010, 2(2): 5299-5303.

[2] ATCHISON J. Aitchison's Linguistics: Teach Yourself[M]. London: Hodder Education, 1999.

[3] AUFA F. The use of discourse completion task (DCT) as explicit instruction on indonesian EFL learners' production of suggestion acts[J]. International Journal on Studies in English Language and Literature (IJSELL), 2014, 2(6): 1-10.

[4] BANDURA A. Self-efficacy: toward a unifying theory of behavioral change[J]. Psychological review, 1977, 84(2): 191-215.

[5] BANDURA A. Social foundations of thought and action: A social cognitive theory[M]. Englewood Cliffs, NJ: Prentice-Hall, 1986.

[6] BANDURA A. Social cognitive theory[J]. Annals of child development, 1989, 6: 1-60.

[7] BANDURA A. Social cognitive theory of moral thought and action[M]//W. M. Kurtines & J. L. Gewirtz. Handbook of moral behavior and development. Hillsdale: Erlbaum, 1991a, 45-103.

[8] BANDURA A. Social cognitive theory of self-regulation[J]. Organizational Behavior and Human Decision Processes, 1991b, 50(2): 248-287.

[9] BANDURA A. Self-efficacy [J]. V. S. Ramachaudran. Encyclopedia of Human Behavior, 1994, 4:71-81.

[10] BAUER L. English Word-formation [M]. Cambridge: Oxford University Press, 1983.

[11] BAUER L. Introducing Linguistic Morphology [M]. Edinburgh: Edinburgh University Press, 1988.

[12] BAUMAN R. Story, Performance and Event[M]. Cambridge: Cambridge University Press, 1986.

[13] BAUMANR, BRIGGS C. Poetics and performance as critical Perspectives on language and social life[J]. Annual Review of Anthropology, 1990, 19: 59-88.

[14] BAYS H. Framing and Face in Internet Exchanges: A Socio-Cognitive Approach[J/OL]. Linguistic online, 1998, 1(1). https://bop. unibe. ch/linguistik-online/article/view/1080/1769

[15] BELL N. Formulaic language, creativity, and language play in a second Language [J]. Annual Review of Applied Linguistics, 2012, 32: 189-205.

[16] BHABHA H. Of mimicry and man: The ambivalence of colonial discourse [J]. Discipleship: A Special Issue on Psychoanalysis, 1984, 28(1): 125-133.

[17] BLOCK D. The Social Turn in Second Language Acquisition [M]. Edinburgh: Edinburgh University Press, 2003.

[18] BLOOMFIELD L. Language [M]. New York: Holt, Rinehart & Winston, 1993.

[19] BLUM-KULKA S. Learning how to say what you mean in a second language: A study of Hebrew as a second language [J]. Applied Linguistics, 1982, 3: 29-59.

[20] BODEN M. Dimensions of Creativity [M]. Boston: MIT Press, 1994.

[21] BODEN M. Creativity and knowledge [M]//A. Craft, B.

Jeffery, & M. Leibling. Creativity in Education. London/New York: Continuum, 2001: 95 - 102.

[22] BOHIKEN R, MACIAS L. What a Non-native Speaker of English Needs to Learn through Listening[C]//Conference Paper: Annual Meeting of the International Listening Association, Seattle, Washington, March 5 - 7, 1992. http://files.eric.ed.gov/fulltext/ED350637.pdf

[23] BOLTON K, DAVIS D R. A content analysis of World Englishes[J]. World Englishes, 2006, 25(1): 5 - 6.

[24] BONDI M. "If you think this sounds very complicated, you are correct": awareness of cultural difference in specialized discourse[M]//Christopher N. Candlin, & M. Gotti. Intercultural Aspects of Specialized Communication, Oxford: Peter Lang Bern, 2007, 53 - 78.

[25] BOUVERESSE J. On linguistic methodology[M]//H. Parret. Discussing Language. The Hague: Mouton, 1974: 301 - 403.

[26] BOWN J, WHITE C. A social and cognitive approach to affect in SLA [J]. International Review of Applied Linguistics in Language Teaching, 2010, 48(4): 331 - 353.

[27] BURNEY V H. Applications of social cognitive theory to gifted education[J]. Roeper Review, 2008, 30(2): 130 - 139.

[28] BURTON P. Creativity in Hong Kong schools[J]. World Englishes, 2010, 29(4): 493 - 507.

[29] CARTER R. Common language: corpus, creativity and cognition[J]. Language and literature, 1999, 8(3): 195 - 216.

[30] CARTER R. Language and Creativity: The Art of Common Talk[M]. London/New York: Routledge, 2004.

[31] CARTER R, McCarthy M. Talking, creating: interactional language, creativity, and context[J]. Applied Linguistics, 2004, 25(1): 62 - 88.

[32] CARTER R. Response to special issue of Applied Linguistics devoted to language creativity in everyday contexts [J]. Applied Linguistics，2007，28(4)：597－608.

[33] CHANDRASEGARAN A. The effect of a socio-cognitive approach to teaching writing on stance support moves and topicality in students' expository essays[J]. Linguistics and Education，2013，24(2)：101－111.

[34] CHOMSKY N. A review of B. F. Skinner's verbal behavior [M]//J. A. Fodor & J. J. Katz. The Structure of Language: Readings in the Philosophy of Language. New Jersey: Prentice-Hall，Inc.，Englewood Cliffs，1964a：547－578.

[35] CHOMSKY N. Current Issues in Linguistic Theory[M]. The Hague：Mouton，1964b.

[36] CHOMSKY N. Aspects of the theory of Syntax[M]. Cambridge: The M.I.T. Press，1965.

[37] CHOMSKY N. Cartesian Linguistics: A Chapter in the History of Rationalist Thought[M]. New York & London: Harper & Row，1966.

[38] CHOMSKY N. Language and Mind (2nd edition)[M]. New York：Harcourt Brace Jovanovich，1972.

[39] CHOMSKY N. Dialog with H. Parret [M]//H. Parret. Discussing Language. The Hague：Mouton，1974：27－54.

[40] CHUNG K H. Non-native speaker teachers' professional identities: the effects of teaching experience and linguistic and social contexts[D]. Books & Theses - Gradworks，2014.

[41] COGO A. Intercultural Communication in English as a Lingua Franca：a Case Study[D]. London：King's College，2007.

[42] COGO A. Accommodating difference in EFL conversations: a study of pragmatic strategies[M]//A. Mauranen，E. Ranta. English as a Lingua Franca：Studies and Findings Newcastle upon Tyne：Cambridge Scholars Publishing，2009：254－273.

[43] COGO A. Strategic use and perceptions of English as a Lingua Franca [J]. Poznań Studies in Contemporary Linguistics, 2010, 46(3): 295 - 312.

[44] COGO A. English as a Lingua Franca: concepts, use, and implications[J]. ELT Journal, 2012, 66(1): 97 - 105.

[45] COGO A, Dewey M. Analyzing English as a Lingua Franca: A Corpus-driven Investigation [M]. London: Continuum International Publishing Group, 2012.

[46] COOK G. Language play, language learning [J]. English Language Teaching Journal, 1997, 51(3): 224 - 231.

[47] COOK G. Linguistics and language teaching[M]//K. Johnson H. Johnson. The Encyclopedic of Dictionary of Applied Linguistics. Oxford: Blackwell, 1998: 198 - 207.

[48] COOK G. Language Play, Language Learning[M]. Oxford, UK: Oxford University Press, 2000.

[49] COOK V. Going beyond the native speaker in language teaching[J]. TESOL Quarterly, 1999, 33(2): 185 - 209.

[50] COULMAS F. Conversational Routines: Explorations in Standardized Communicative Situations and Prepatterned Speech[M]. The Hague: Mouton, 1981.

[51] CRYSTAL D. Language Play[M]. Harmondsworth: Penguin, 1998.

[52] CSIKSZENTMIHALYI M. Implications of a system's perspective for the study of creativity[M]//R. J. Sternberg. Handbook of Creativity. Cambridge: Cambridge University Press, 1999: 313 - 335.

[53] DE BEAUGRANDE R. Linguistics and Creativity [C]// Conference Paper: the Interdisciplinary Conference on Linguistics, Louisville, Kentucky, 1978.

[54] DEN OUDEN BERNARD D. Language and Creativity[M]. Lisse: The Peter De Ridder Press, 1975.

[55] DINGS A. Native speaker/non-native speaker interaction and orientation to novice/expert identity[J]. Journal of Pragmatics，2012，44(11)：1503－1518.

[56] DURANTI A，Goodwin C. Rethinking Context：Language as an Interactive Phenomenon[M]. New York：Cambridge University Press，1992.

[57] ELLIS Rod. The study of second language acquisition[M]. Oxford：Oxford University Press，1994.

[58] ERLICH R J，RUSS-EFT D. Applying social cognitive theory to academic advising to assess student learning outcomes[J]. Nacada Journal，2011，31(2)：5－15.

[59] ERLICH R J，RUSS-EFT D. Assessing student learning in academic advising using social cognitive theory[J]. Nacada Journal，2013，33(1)：16－33.

[60] EUN B. The Impact of an English as a Second Language Professional Development Program：A Social Cognitive Approach[D]. Chapel Hill：University of North Carolina，2006.

[61] EVANS V. Lexical concepts，cognitive models and meaning-construction[J]. Cognitive Linguistics，2006，7(4)：491－534.

[62] FINKE R A. Imagery，creativity，and emergent structure[J]. Consciousness and Cognition：An International Journal，1996，5(3)：381－393.

[63] FIRTH A，WAGNER J. On discourse，communication，and (some) fundamental concepts in SLA research[J]. The Modem Language Journal，1997，81(3)：286－300.

[64] FISHER R. Critical creativity：A study of ‘Political Correct’ terms in style guides for different types of discourse[M]//J. Munat. Lexical Creativity，Texts and Contexts. Amsterdam/Philadelphia：John Benjamins Publishing Company，2007：

263 - 282.

[65] FLOWERDEW J. Attitudes of journal editors to non-native speaker contributions[J]. TESOL Quarterly, 2001, 35(1): 121 - 150.

[66] D'AGOSTINO F. Chomsky on Creativity [J]. Synthese, 1984, 58(1): 85 - 117.

[67] FUNK, WAGNALLS COMPANY. Comprehensive Standard International Dictionary[M], 1973.

[68] FUSHS B. Mimesis and Empire: The New World, Islam and European Identities[M]. Cambridge: Cambridge University Press, 2001.

[69] GARCIA M J B, TERKOURAFI M. First-order politeness in rapprochement and distance cultures: understandings and uses of politeness by Spanish native speakers from Spain and Spanish non-native speakers from the US[J]. Pragmatics, 2014, 24(1): 1 - 34

[70] GAVIN J, STEEN G. Cognitive Poetics in Practice[M]. London: HarperCollins, 2003.

[71] GAY W. Analogy and metaphor: two models of linguistic creativity[J]. Philosophy and Social Criticism, 1980, 7(3/4): 299 - 317.

[72] GEE J P. An Introduction to Discourse Analysis: Theory and method[M]. New York/London: Routledge, 1999.

[73] GERRING R, GIBBS R J. Beyond the lexicon: creativity in language production[J]. Metaphor and Symbolic Activity, 1988, 3(1): 1 - 19.

[74] GOFFMAN E. Frame Analysis: An Essay on the Organization of Experience[M]. New York: Harper and Row, 1974.

[75] GONZALEZ L M. College-level choice of Latino high school students: A social-cognitive approach [J]. Journal of Multicultural Counseling and Development, 2012, 40(3):

144－155.

[76] GRICE H P. Logic and conversation[M]//P. Cole and J. Morgan. Studies in Syntax and Semantics III：Speech Acts. New York：Academic Press，1975：183－198.

[77] GUPTA N. Creativity and values：educational perspectives [M]. New Delhi：Arya Book Depot，1992.

[78] HADI A. A critical appraisal of Crice's Cooperative Principle [J]. Open Journal of Modern Linguistics，2013，3(1)：69－72.

[79] HALLIDAY M A K. Explorations in the Functions of Language[M]. London：Arnold，1973.

[80] HALLIDAY M A K，HASAN R. Cohesion in English[M]. Longman：Longmans，1976.

[81] HALLIDAY M A K，MCLNTOSH A.，STREVENS P. The Linguistic Sciences and Language Teaching[M]. London：Longmans，1964.

[82] HAMID M O，BOLDAUF JR R B. Second language errors and features of World Englishes[J]. World Englishes，2013，32(4)：476－494.

[83] HASHIM A，BENNUI P. Lexical creativity in Thai English fiction[J]. Kritika Kultura，2013，(21/22)：132－163.

[84] HAWLEY L，HARKER D，HARKER M. A social cognitive approach to tackle inactivity and obesity in young Australians [J]. Journal of Business Research，2010，63(2)：116－120.

[85] HERNÁNDEZ-CAMPOY J M，CUTILLAS-ESPINOSA J A. The effects of public and individual language attitudes on intra-speaker variation：A Case Study of Style-shifting[J]. Multilingua，2013，32(1)：79－101.

[86] HOHENHAUS P. How to do (even more) things with inonce words (other than naming) [M]//MUNAT J. Lexical Creativity，Texts and Contexts. Amsterdam/Philadelphia：

John Benjamins Publishing Company, 2007: 15 - 38.

[87] HOLT E B, BROWN H C. Animal Drive and the Learning Process: An Essay Toward Radical Empiricism[M]. New York: H. Holt and Co, 1931.

[88] HOUSE J. Misunderstanding in intercultural communication: Interactions in English as lingua franca and the myth of mutual intelligibility [M]//C. Gnutzmann. Teaching and Learning English as a Global Language. Tubingen: Stauffenburg, 1999: 73 - 89.

[89] HOUSE J. Subjectivity in English as lingua franca discourse: the case of you know[J]. Intercultural Pragmatics, 2009, 6(2): 171 - 93.

[90] HUDSON G. Essential Introductory Linguistics[M]. Malden, Mass: Blackwell, 2000.

[91] HULMBAUER C. "We don't take the right way. We just take the way that we think you will understand" — The shifting relationship between correctness and effectiveness [M]//A. Mauranen & E. Ranta. English as a Lingua Franca: Studies and Findings. Newcastle upon Tyne: Cambridge Scholars Publishing, 2009: 323 - 347.

[92] HUTTNER J. Fluent speaker — fluent interaction: on the creation of (co)- fluency in English as a lingua franca[M]// A. Mauranen, E. Ranta. English as a Lingua Franca: Studies and Findings. Newcastle upon Tyne: Cambridge Scholars Publishing, 2009: 274 - 297.

[93] JAKOBSON J. Closing statement: linguistics and poetics [M]//Sebeok, T. A. Style in Language. Cambridge: M.I.T. Press, 1960: 350 - 377.

[94] JEBAHI K. Tunisian university students' choice of apology strategies in a discourse completion task [J]. Journal of Pragmatics, 2011, 43(2): 648 - 662.

[95] JOHN D A F，DUMANIG F P，ACKERMANN K. Language choice，code switching and identity construction in Malaysian English newspaper advertisements[J]. Language in India，2014，14(8)：10－16.

[96] JOHNSOM M. The Body in the Mind：The Bodily Basis of Reason and the Imagination[M]. Chicago：University of Chicago Press，1987.

[97] JONES R H. Creativity and discourse[J]. World Englishes，2010，29(4)：467－480.

[98] KASPER G. Data collection in pragmatics[M]//SPENCER-OATEY H. Culturally Speaking. London：Continuum，2000：316－341.

[99] KAUR J. Intercultural communication in English as a lingua franca：Some sources of misunderstanding[J]. Intercultural Pragmatics，2011，8(1)：93－116.

[100] KECSKES I. A cognitive-pragmatic approach to situation-bound utterances[J]. Journal of Pragmatics，2000，32(6)：605－625.

[101] KECSKES I. Situation-Bound Utterances in L1 and L2[M]. Berlin/New York：Mouton de Gruyter，2003.

[102] KECSKES I. Dueling contexts：A dynamic model of meaning[J]. Journal of Pragmatics，2008，40(3)：385－406.

[103] KECSKES I. The paradox of communication：Socio-cognitive approach to pragmatics[J]. Pragmatics and Society，2010a，1(1)：50－73.

[104] KECSKES I. Dual and multilanguage systems[J]. International Journal of Multilingualism，2010b，7(2)：91－109.

[105] KECSKES I. Is there anyone out there who really is interested in the speaker? [J] Language and Dialogue，2012，2(2)：283－297.

[106] KECSKES I. Intercultural Pragmatics[M]. Oxford, UK: Oxford University Press, 2013a.

[107] KECSKES I. Why do we say what we say the way we say it? [J]. Journal of Pragmatics, 2013b, 48(1): 71 - 83.

[108] KECSKES I, ZHANG F. Activating, seeking, and creating common ground[J]. Pragmatics and Cognition, 2009, 17 (2): 331 - 355.

[109] KEYSAR B, HENLY A S. Speakers' overestimation of their effectiveness[J]. Psychological Science, 2002, 13(3): 207 - 212.

[110] KHATIB M, SHAKOURI N. On situating the stance of socio-cognitive approach to language acquisition[J]. Theory and Practice in Language Studies, 2013, 3(9): 1590 - 1595.

[111] KIM H, PHELPS J E, LEE D. The Social Cognitive Approach to Consumers' Engagement Behavior in Online Brand Community[J]. International Journal of Integrated Marketing Communication, 2013, 5(2): 7 - 22.

[112] KIM K, LEE Y, LEE C H. College students' style of language usage: clues to creativity [J]. Perceptual and Motor Skills, 2012, 114(1): 43 - 50.

[113] KLIMPFINGER T. "She's mixing the two languages together" — Forms and functions of code-switching in English as a lingua franca[M]//MAURANEN A, RANTA E. English as a Lingua Franca: Studies and Findings. Newcastle upon Tyne: Cambridge Scholars Publishing, 2009: 348 - 371.

[114] KOESTLER A. The Art of Creation[M]. London: Hutchinson, 1964.

[115] KOLLER V. How to analyze collective identity in discourse — Textual and contextual parameters [J]. Critical Approaches to Discourse Analysis across Disciplines, 2012,

5(2)：19－38.

[116] KRAMSCH C. Guest Column：The privilege of the non-native speaker [J]. Modern Language Association of America，1997，112(3)：359－369.

[117] KRAMSCH C. Second language acquisition，applied linguistics and the teaching of foreign language[J]. The Language Learning Journal，2007，27(1)：66－73.

[118] KRESS G. Literacy in the New Media Age[M]. London：Routledge，2003.

[119] KUIPER K. Cathy Wilcox meets the phrasal lexicon：creative deformation of phrasal lexical items for humorous effect[M]//MUNAT J. Lexical Creativity，Texts and Contexts. Amsterdam/Philadelphia：John Benjamins Publishing Company，2007：93－114.

[120] LAKOFF G，JOHNSON M. Philosophy in the Flesh：The Embodied Mind and Its Challenge to Western Thought[M]. Chicago：University of Chicago Press，1999.

[121] LANTOLF J. The function of language play in the acquisition of L2 Spanish[M]//GLASS W. R.，PEREZ-LEROUX A. T. Contemporary Perspectives on the Acquisition of Spanish. Somerville：Cascadilla Press，1997：2－24.

[122] LEE D，LAROSE R. The impact of personalized social cues of immediacy on consumers' information disclosure：A social cognitive approach[J]. Cyberpsychology，Behavior，and Social Networking，2011，14(6)：337－343.

[123] LEE E J. Exploring L2 Writing Strategies from a Socio-cognitive Perspective：Mediated Actions，Goals，and Setting in L2 Writing[D]. Columbus：The Ohio State University，2011.

[124] LEHRER A. Blendalicious[M]//MUNAT J. Lexical Creativity，Texts and Contexts. Amsterdam/Philadelphia：John Benjamins

Publishing Company, 2007: 115 - 136.

[125] LENT R W, BROWN S D, HACKETT G. Toward a unifying social cognitive theory of career and academic interest, choice, and performance[J]. Journal of Vocational Behavior, 1994, 45(1): 79 - 122.

[126] LIN A. The bilingual verbal art of frame: Linguistic hybridity and creativity of a Hong Kong hip-hop group [M]//SWANN J, POPE R, CARTER R. Creativity in Language and Literature: The State of the Art. London: Palgrave Macmillan, 2011: 55 - 67.

[127] LINELL Per. Approaching Dialogue: Talk and interaction in dialogical perspectives[M]. Linkoping: Department of Communication Studies, 1996.

[128] LIPKA L. Metaphor und Metonymie—Pozesse, Resultate und ihre Besch-reibung [J]. Munstersches Logbuch zur Linguistic, 1994, 5: 1 - 13.

[129] LIPKA L. English Lexicology: Lexical Structure, Word Semantics, and Word-formation [M]. Tubingen: Gunter Narr, 2002.

[130] LIPKA L. Lexical creativity, textuality and problems of metalanguage[M]//MUNAT J. Lexical Creativity, Texts and Contexts. Amsterdam/Philadelphia: John Benjamins Publishing Company, 2007: 3 - 14.

[131] LIU D, GLEASON J L. Acquisition of the article "The" by non-native speakers of English: An analysis of four nongeneric uses[J]. Studies in Second Language Acquisition, 2002, 24(1): 1 - 26.

[132] LOPEZ RUA P. Keeping up with the items: Lexical creativity in electronic communication [M]//MUNAT J. Lexical Creativity, Texts and Contexts. Amsterdam/ Philadelphia: John Benjamins Publishing Company, 2007:

137－162.

[133] LOW B, SHAKAR M, WINTER L. 'Ch'us mon propre Bescherelle': Challenges from the Hip-Hop nation to the Quebec nation[J]. Journal of Sociolinguistics, 2009, 13(1): 59－82.

[134] LUMSDEN D. Kinds of conversational cooperation[J]. Journal of Pragmatics, 2008, 40(11): 1896－1908.

[135] MAGNUSSON L. Shakespeare and Social Dialogue: Dramatic Language and Elizabethan Letters [M]. Cambridge: Cambridge University Press, 1999.

[136] MANTYSALO R. Dilemmas in critical planning theory[J]. Town Planning Review, 2002, 73(4): 417－438.

[137] MAURANEN A. Chunking in ELF: expressions for managing interaction[J]. Journal of Intercultural Pragmatics, 2009, 6(2): 217－233.

[138] MAYBIN J, SWANN J. Everyday creativity in language: textuality, contextuality, and critique [J]. Applied Linguistics, 2007, 28(4): 497－517.

[139] MENSAH E, NDIMELE R. Linguistic creativity in Nigerian pidgin advertising[J]. Sociolinguistic Studies, 2013, 7(3): 321－344.

[140] MILLER N E, DOLLARD J. Social learning and imitation [M]. New Haven: Yale University Press, 1941.

[141] MONEY W H. Applying group support systems to classroom settings: A social cognitive learning theory explanation[J]. Journal of Management Information Systems, 1995, 12(3): 65－80.

[142] MORRIS C A W, SHOFFNER M F, NEWSOME D W. Career counseling for women preparing to leave abusive relationships: a social cognitive career theory approach[J]. Career Development Quarterly, 2009, 58(1): 44－53.

[143] MUNRO M J, DERWING T M, BURGESS C S. Detection of non-native speaker status from content-masked speech [J]. Speech Communication, 2010, 52 (7): 626 - 637.

[144] NORRICK N. Conversational Narrative[M]. Amsterdam: John Benjamins Publishing Company, 2000.

[145] NORTH S. 'The Voices, the Voices': Creativity in online conversation[M]. Applied Linguistics, 2007, 28(4): 538 - 555.

[146] NUYTS J. Aspects of a Cognitive-Pragmatic Theory of Language [M]. Amsterdam: John Benjamins Publishing Company, 1992.

[147] OSVALDSSON K, PERSSON-THUNQVIST D, CROMDAL J. Comprehension checks, clarifications, and corrections in an emergency call with a non-native speaker of Swedish. International Journal of Bilingualism, 2013, 17(2): 205 - 220.

[148] PAE H K, GREENBERG D. The relationship between receptive and expressive subskills of academic L2 proficiency in non-native speakers of English: A multigroup approach[J]. Reading Psychology, 2014, 35(3): 221 - 259.

[149] PARADIS M. Cerebral division of labour in verbal communication [M]//SANDRA D, OSTMAN JO, VERSCHUEREN J. Cognition and Pragmatics. Amsterdam: John Benjamins Publishing Company, 2009: 53 - 77.

[150] PARK G. "I Am Never Afraid of Being Recognized as an NNES": One teacher's journey in claiming and embracing her non-native-speaker identity [J]. TESOL QUARTERLY, 2012, 46(1): 127 - 151.

[151] PARVARESH V, TAVAKOLI M. Discourse completion tasks as elicitation tools: How convergent are they? [J]. The Social Science, 2009, 4(4): 366 - 373.

[152] PATRICK H. How to say new things：An essay on linguistic creativity[J]. Brno Study in English，2008，57(14)：39－50.

[153] PAVLENKO A. "I'm Very Not about the Law Part"：Non-native speakers of English and the Miranda Warnings[J]，TESOL Quarterly，2008，42(1)：1－30.

[154] PAWLEY A，SYDER F H. Two puzzles for linguistic theory：Nativelike selection and nativelike fluency[M]// RICHARDS J，SCHMITT R. W. Language and Communication. London：Routledge，1983：191－226.

[155] PENNYCOOK A. "The rotation gets thick. The constraints get thin"：Creativity，recontextualization，and difference [J]. Applied Linguistics，2007，28(4)：579－596.

[156] PILLER I. Intercultural Communication：A Critical Introduction [M]. Edinburgh：Edinburgh University Press，2011.

[157] PITZL M L. "We should not wake up any dogs"：Idiom and metaphor in EFL [M]//MAURANEN A，RANTA E. English as a Lingua Franca：Studies and Findings. Newcastle upon Tyne：Cambridge Scholars Publishing，2009：298－322.

[158] POPE R. Creativity：Theory，History，Practice[M]. London：Routledge，2005.

[159] POPE R. Rewriting the critical-creative continuum："10x . . ." [M]//SWANN J，POPE R，CARTER R. Creativity in Language and Literature：The State of the Art. London：Palgrave Macmillan，2011，250－264.

[160] POPE R，SWANN J. Introduction：creativity，language，literature [M]//SWANN J，POPE R，CARTER R. Creativity in Language and Literature：The State of the Art. London：Palgrave Macmillan，2011：1－22.

[161] PRABHAKARAN R，GREEN A E，GRAY J R. Thin slices of creativity：using single-word utterances to assess creative

cognition[J]. Behavior Research Methods, 2014, 46(3): 641-659.

[162] PRATI G. A social cognitive learning theory of homophobic aggression among adolescents [J]. School Psychology Review, 2012, 41(4): 413-428.

[163] PRATT M L. Toward a Speech Act Theory of Literary Discourse [M]. Bloomington: Indiana University Press, 1977.

[164] PREVIGNANO C L, LUZIO A D. A discussion with John J. Gumperz[M]//EERDMANS SUSAN L, PREVIGNANO C L, THIBAULT P J. Language and Interaction—Discussions with John J. Gumperz. Amersterdam/ Philadelphia: John Benjamins Publishing Company, 2003: 7-29.

[165] PRODROMOU L. English as a Lingua Franca: A corpus based analysis[M]. London: Continuum, 2008.

[166] PRODROMOU L. Bumping into creative idiomaticity[M]// COOK G, NORTH S. Applied Linguistics in Action: A Reader. London: Routledge, 2010: 231-245.

[167] RAMPTON B. Crossing: Language and Ethnicity among Adolescents[M]. Manchester: St Jerome Press, 2005.

[168] RHODES M. An analysis of creativity [J]. Phi Delta Kappan, 1961, 42(7): 305-311.

[169] RISKIND J H, BOMBARDIER M, AYERS C. Perceiving normality in clients as a potent social—cognitive treatment approach [J]. Journal of Social and Clinical Psychology, 2006, 25(3): 249-260.

[170] ROACH P. Phonetics [M]. Oxford: Oxford University Press, 2001.

[171] ROBBINS S. Beauty in Language: Tolkien's Phonology and Phonaesthetics as a Source of Creativity and Inspiration for the Lord of the Rings[J]. Zmogus ir Zodis, 2013, 15(1):

183－191.

[172] ROH S B. Toward a Reconceptualization of the Integration of Culture and Language in the Korean EFL Classroom[D]. Seoul：Chung-ang University，2001.

[173] ROJAS-DRUMMOND S M，ALBARRÁN C D，LITTLETON K S. Collaboration，creativity and the co-construction of oral and written texts[J]. Thinking Skills and Creativity，2008，3(3)：177－191.

[174] ROMMETVEIT R. Outlines of a dialogically based social-cognitive approach to human cognition and communication [M]//HEEN W A. The Dialogical Alternative：Towards a theory of language and mind. Oslo：Scandinavian University Press，1992：19－44.

[175] SAMPSON G. Liberty and Language[M]. Oxford：Oxford University Press，1979.

[176] SAMPSON G. Making Sense[M]. Oxford：Oxford University Press，1980.

[177] SEIDLHOFER B. Research perspectives on reaching English as a lingua franca[J]. Annual Review of Applied Linguistics，2004，24(1)：209－239.

[178] SHERZER J. Speech Play and Verbal Art[M]. Austin：University of Texas Press，2002.

[179] SIMPSON P，HALL G. Discourse Analysis and Stylistics[J]. Annual Review of Applied Linguistics，2002，22(1)：134－149.

[180] SKINNER B F. Verbal Behavior[M]. Acton：Copley Publishing Group，1957.

[181] STEIN S M，HARPER T L. Creativity and innovation：Divergence and convergence in pragmatic and dialogical planning[J]. Journal of Planning Education and Research，2012，32(1)：5－17.

[182] SWANN J. The art of the everyday[M]//MAYBIN J, SWANN J. The Art of English: Everyday English. Glasgow: CPI, 2006: 3-53.

[183] SWANN J, MAYBIN J. Introduction: Language creativity in everyday contexts[J]. Applied Linguistics, 2007, 28(4): 491-496.

[184] SWANN J, POPE R, CARTER R. Creativity in Language and Literature: The State of the Art[M]. London: Palgrave Macmillan, 2011.

[185] SYNDER M. On the self-perpetuating nature of social stereotypes[M]//HAMILTON D L. Cognitive Processes in Stereotyping and Intergroup Behavior. Hillsdale: Erlbaum, 1981: 182-212.

[186] TALEGHANI-NIKAZM C. A conversation analytical study of telephone conversation openings between native and non-native speakers[J]. Journal of Pragmatics, 2002, 34(12): 1807-1832.

[187] TANNEN D. Talking Voices: Repetition, Dialogue and Imagery in Conversational Discourse[M]. Cambridge: Cambridge University Press, 1989.

[188] TAUSSIG M. Mimesis and Alterity: A Particular History of the Senses[M]. New York: Routledge, 1993.

[189] THOGERSEN J, GRONHOJ A. Electricity saving in households—A social cognitive approach[J]. Energy Policy, 2010, 38(12): 7732-7743.

[190] TIN T B. Language creativity and co-emergence of form and meaning in creative writing tasks[J]. Applied Linguistics, 2011, 32(2): 215-235.

[191] TSAKONA V. Linguistic creativity and institutional design—the case of Greek parliamentary discourse[J]. Byzantine and Modern Greek Studies, 2012, 36 (1): 91-109.

[192] VAN LANCKER-SIDTIS D, RALLON G. Tracking the incidence of formulaic expressions in everyday speech: Methods for classification and verification[J]. Language and Communication, 2004, 24(3): 207-240.

[193] VEALE T, BUTNARIU C. Exploring linguistic creativity via predictive lexicology[M/OL]//COLTON S, ALISON P. The Third Joint Workshop on Computational Creativity. Trento: Universita di Trento, 2006. http://ccg.doc.gold.ac.uk/events/ecai06/proceedings/Veale.pdf

[194] VEGA-MORENO R E. Creativity and Convention: The Pragmatics of Everyday Figurative Speech[M]. Amsterdam/Philadelphia: John Benjamins Publishing Company, 2007.

[195] VETTOREL P, FRANCESCHI V. English and lexical inventiveness in the Italian linguistic landscape[J]. English Text Construction, 2013, 6(2): 238-270.

[196] VOICE. The Vienna-Oxford International Corpus of English (version 2.0 online). Director: Barbara Seidlhofer; Researchers: Angelika Breiteneder, Theresa Klimpfinger, Stefan Majewski, Ruth Osimk-Teasdale, Marie-Luise Pitzl, Michael Radeka[EB/OL]. http://voice.univie.ac.at, 2013.

[197] WARD T B, SMITH S M, VAID J. Creative Thought: An Investigation of Conceptual Structures and Processes[M]. Washington: American Psychological Association, 1997.

[198] WOLD A H. The Dialogical Alternative: Towards a theory of language and mind[M]. Oslo: Scandinavian University Press, 1992.

[199] WRAY A. Formulaic language[J]. Language Teaching, 2013, 46(3): 316-334.

[200] WU Y, CHEN V H H. A social-cognitive approach to online game cheating[J]. Computers in Human Behavior, 2013, 29(6): 2557-2567.

[201] XIA S H. Pragmatic skills as reflected in phone conversations: A socio-cognitive inquiry into native/non-native speaker interactions[D]. Albany: State University of New York, 2006.

[202] YANG X M, XU H X. Errors of Creativity[M]. New York: University Press of America, 2001.

[203] YOUNG H N, DILWORTH T J, MOTT D A, et al., Pharmacists' provision of information to Spanish-speaking patients: A social cognitive approach[J]. Research in Social and Administrative Pharmacy, 2013, 9(1): 4-12.

[204] ZAWADA B. Linguistic Creativity and Mental Representation with Reference to Intercategorial Polysemy[D]. Pretoria: University of South Africa, 2005.

[205] ZAWADA B. Linguistic creativity from a cognitive perspective[J]. Southern African Linguistics and Applie0d Language Studies, 2006, 24(2): 235-254.

[206] ZUSKIN R D. Assessing L2 sociolinguistic competence: In search of support from pragmatic theories[J]. Pragmatics and Language Learning, 1993, 4: 166-182.

[207] 黄也平,侯盼.网络语言对现代汉语的创新及其反思[J].江西社会科学,2012,(3):238-241.

[208] 刘辰诞.边界移动:语言创新的一个动因[J].外语学刊,2012,(1):30-34.

[209] 刘正光,刘润清.语言非范畴化理论的意义[J].外语教学与研究(外国语文双月刊),2005,37(1):29-37.

[210] 石岩.修辞视角下的语言创新性[J].河北理工大学学报(社会科学版),2008,8(3):84-87.

[211] 苏晓玉.计算机语言中的文学隐喻与语言创新特征[J].解放军外国语学院学报,1999,22(5):28-31.

[212] 汤玫英.网络语言创新的动因及其不当取向[J].河南师范大学学报(哲学社会科学版),2010,(4):181-184.